Calling a Snow Day

Calling a Snow Day

How Local Politics Influence School Decisions

Richard D. Tomko

ROWMAN & LITTLEFIELD
Lanham • Boulder • New York • London

Published by Rowman & Littlefield
An imprint of The Rowman & Littlefield Publishing Group, Inc.
4501 Forbes Boulevard, Suite 200, Lanham, Maryland 20706
www.rowman.com

86-90 Paul Street, London EC2A 4NE

Copyright © 2024 by Richard D. Tomko

All rights reserved. No part of this book may be reproduced in any form or by any electronic or mechanical means, including information storage and retrieval systems, without written permission from the publisher, except by a reviewer who may quote passages in a review.

British Library Cataloguing in Publication Information Available

Library of Congress Cataloging-in-Publication Data

Names: Tomko, Richard D., 1973- author.
Title: Calling a snow day : how local politics influence school decisions / Richard D. Tomko.
Description: Lanham, Maryland : Rowman & Littlefield, [2024] | Summary: "Calling a Snow Day: How Local Politics Influence School Decisions is a tool to help leaders in education identify, understand, and be able to maneuver around any and all obstacles that would influence decisions based on the needs of the constituent and stakeholder group and not just the system as a whole"— Provided by publisher.
Identifiers: LCCN 2024027914 (print) | LCCN 2024027915 (ebook) | ISBN 9781475872101 (cloth) | ISBN 9781475872118 (paperback) | ISBN 9781475872125 (epub)
Subjects: LCSH: Education—Political aspects—United States. | Weather—Political aspects—United States. | Education and state—United States. | Educational leadership—United States. | Educational accountability—United States.
Classification: LCC LC89 .T66 2024 (print) | LCC LC89 (ebook) | DDC 379.73—dc23/eng/20240628
LC record available at https://lccn.loc.gov/2024027914
LC ebook record available at https://lccn.loc.gov/2024027915

Dedication

This manuscript and the meaning beyond its pages are dedicated to my beautiful wife, Jaimie. We have spent our entire married lives in the administrative space, and you have lived through the trials and tribulations of being an educational administrator with me each and every day. From the "all hours" of the evening calls from board members, to working during family vacations, my missing important events due to a scheduling conflict with a district concert or activity, to the late-night monitoring of weather reports when an impending snowstorm was approaching—you never once complained, and you always supported me and what I had to do to be successful in my career. I absolutely owe my career trajectory to the unwavering support you have shown me every minute of every day.

But most of all, you have been a partner to me—my true consigliere—during all the political battles, losses, and triumphs throughout all these years. Without you by my side, I wouldn't have made it this far and would still be lost.

Although I know I will never be able to repay you for all you have done for me, my promise to you is that I will try my best for the rest of my life to do so.

I continue to fall in love with you over and over again with each new day.

You are an incredible wife, mother, and my best friend. For this and much more, I continue to be in awe of how you make everyone around you feel without ever thinking of yourself first.

You are and will always be my inspiration.

—RT
Nunc scio quid sit amor

Legal Disclaimer

This text has been written as an advisory and teaching tool for professors, current and aspiring educational leaders, and those individuals they serve. Professionals should always check with legal counsel prior to making any decisions that may impact a school, district, or organization.

Contents

Acknowledgment		xi
Educational Leadership Defined		xiii
You Make the Call!		xv
The Coaches' Corner		xvii
1	Calling a Snow Day	1
2	The Decision-Making Process	5
3	Influencing Matters	17
4	Avoiding the Political Tsunami	27
5	Navigating Local Politics	37
6	Considerations for Polioptics in Local Decision Making	45
7	Forming Local Alliances	51
8	Building Partnerships	57
9	Directed Informational Leadership	65
10	Stakeholders as Defined in Educational Settings	71
11	How to Engage Stakeholder Groups	81
12	The Importance of Feedforward and Feedback Loops	85
13	Gadflies	91
14	How to Spot Political Machines	95

15	Surveying and Surviving Political Trends	99
16	The Playbook of Politics for Educational Leaders	105
17	The Importance of Protecting Others	109
18	Transparency 101	113
19	Et tu, Brute?	117
20	Knowing When to Exit and Planning It	121

| About the Author | 129 |

Acknowledgment

This manuscript was written to acknowledge the numerous educational leaders I have mentored over my past twenty-five years in educational administration and who have remained close colleagues with me throughout my journey. Although we make each day look easy, we all know that the individuals we serve who respect us today can be the same individuals who believe someone else can do it better tomorrow.

And although we report to our positions every day because of our calling to serve the youth of the world, to make a brighter tomorrow as we turn learners into leaders, it's not an easy road to travel.

But for those who make it to the end of the journey, the reward is priceless.

Educational Leadership Defined

Throughout the text, you will see references to different titles that correspond to different educational leadership positions. In 2022, there were 285,910 education administrators (K–12) in the United States.[1] Although each state, county, and local education agency (LEA) has its own set of statutes and rules governing position controls and certification matrices for school leadership licensure, the functions, duties, and responsibilities are generally the same in any educational leadership position across the country.

In the subsequent chapters of the text, each educational setting (whether private/public or charter primary, secondary, or higher education) that is described is defined as a district, school, or organization. At times, references are also made to the educational system as a whole. These terms represent any education system supervised by any individual who serves in an educational leadership role.

Also within each chapter, references to individuals who serve in these leadership roles carry titles that include, but are not limited to:

- educational leader
- administrator
- school leader
- superintendent of schools
- chief school administrator (CSA)
- school chief
- director
- principal
- assistant principal
- supervisor
- chief officer

Although each of these positions will host different responsibilities, and supervisory and evaluator powers, inside different organizational charts pursuant to the district, school, or organization they serve, their titles are synonymous with the tenets of educational leadership and the political landscape each will face when making local decisions.

ENDNOTE

[1] U.S. Bureau of Labor Statistics. (2022). 11-9032 Education Administrators, Kindergarten through Secondary.

You Make the Call!

Each chapter includes a "You Make the Call!" (YMTC) section to help foster an educated discussion about the main theme of the current and previous chapters. The section includes an in-box scenario based loosely on a factual situation that occurred in a school, district, or organization.

The purpose of the scenario and section is to assist in facilitating a dialogue that will place the reader inside the scenario and prompt her to make decisions based on past knowledge, school law, her moral compass, and—most importantly—common sense.

Conversations around the YMTC scenarios should include academic, legal, ethical, policy, and political considerations on how best to complete the scenario or how an individual could have handled the situation differently. Facilitators can easily add to the scenarios and lead the outcome in different directions to create a deeper dive into the theme of the chapter.

It is important to note that although there may be legal, ethical, and statutory issues inside these scenarios that would prompt absolute right or wrong answers, many actions that administrators take in actual scenarios are based on the culture of the individual school, district, or organization and the political landscape of the system when the scenario is occurring. In stating this, each scenario will be handled differently pertinent to the who, what, and where that surrounds the incident taking place.

As always, educational leaders should consult with legal counsel prior to making any decision that may impact the school system as a whole or the leader individually.

The Coaches' Corner

The Coaches' Corner that concludes each chapter provides follow-up questions to generate further discussions, review educational administrative theory, and provide other real-life scenarios for readers to analyze. Students, district teams, and aspiring leaders may consider using this section of the text to formulate alternative actions to the prescribed scenarios and indicate the potential strengths and weaknesses in the implied leadership strategies for each potential outcome.

Chapter 1

Calling a Snow Day

I think anyone can easily recall the excitement and anxiousness felt as a child when the possibility of a snow day was on the horizon. I remember growing up in the seventies and sitting by the radio at 6 a.m. listening to the news anchor read off the school closings one by one. Today, a robocall, text message, or email notifies the masses that a snow event has caused a district to delay its opening, dismiss early, or cancel school altogether.

Believe it or not, calling a snow day is very stressful for an educational leader. It may be one of the most stressful processes a school leader engages in during her career. The decision itself impacts many moving parts and affects the actions of multiple stakeholder groups.

Overall, the decision-making process in educational leadership can be considered unique in the eyes of outsiders to the field of educational leadership, management, and policy. In fact, what seem to be simple or obvious decisions to those community stakeholders usually have unexpected outcomes. To be frank, decisions that educational leaders make—even decisions made with input from the stakeholders and backed by data and evidence—are most always scrutinized and criticized by some portion of the community one serves. If a leader can't anticipate making half of his constituents upset at his decision at least half the time, then he still has a long way to go to become a successful leader.

The decision-making process in educational leadership is vitally important due to its wide-reaching impact on students, teachers, the entire education system, and the serving community, township, or city. Seemingly simple or obvious decisions can have unexpected outcomes because of the complexity of the surrounding environment and the potential for unintended consequences. Therefore, educational leaders must approach decision making with care, consideration, and a focus on long-term goals and the well-being of all stakeholders.

IT'S SNOWING!

The anticipation of snow for school-age children creates an interesting euphoria for many reasons including the potential for a day off from school. Even many teachers and administrators are excited at the potential for an extended weekend or a midweek vacation. For the district's chief, excitement is the furthest thing from her mind as she waits, watches, and tracks the impending storm and the looming preparations and decisions that must be made in a specific and short time frame. Alongside the wait comes the inevitable realization that her decisions over the next several hours will never—and I mean *never*—make everyone happy.

Inevitably, most superintendents or chief school administrators will band together during a weather event, making the same decision to stay open, delay, or close using a strength-in-numbers approach. As the hours that school will open draw closer, the communication intensifies until that final decision is made.

For parents, students, and staff members alike, the process seems simple—wake up a little early, look outside the window, and make the call. However, the process itself is much more involved and includes different considerations relative to more than just the safe operation of the schools.

In fact, the process of calling a snow day can be seen as the model for school administrators to use when making any decision that necessitates taking the needs of many, if not all, district stakeholders into consideration.

Although the general public perceives that a school chief looks out her window, makes a few calls, and decides whether to report to work, the thought process is much more defined. Simply put, it really has little to do with the precipitation itself. That's the easy part. If the early morning starts, and three inches of snow are on the ground, it's time to make the call and get the sleds ready.

The real anxiety and difficult choices come during impending forecasts; knowing whether the town can get the streets ready in time; bus and travel safety; possible storm conditions; and day care for students whose parents still need to work. If the township clerk or OEM (Office of Emergency Management) officials call in workers for overtime to get the streets cleaned and salted so that a district can open school . . . well, the chief administrator better open school. Many layers of action and reaction need to be considered when making this type of decision.

This is the exact case with most decisions that a school administrator will make throughout his or her career. The perception of what has occurred sometimes outweighs the reality. This usually holds true because the administrator most times can't explain every facet of a decision or is not allowed to discuss the most intimate details of the situation at hand and what caused the decision due to personnel, student, or legal considerations.

In fact, one can argue that a majority of new members come to this epiphany the first time they sit on a board of education and vote on a recommendation while (for the first time) having all the necessary details to make an informed decision. Prior to that, the board member was sitting anxiously in the audience coming to his own conclusions based on having only one "side" of the story, limited information, and forming his opinion of the matter at hand and the individuals involved. Now, he must sit on a dais and represent his constituent base making decisions that may include only a knowledge base that he has as a current board member. Hence, as decisions are made in the best interest of students, faculty, and staff members with safety always a top priority, many other factors can cause a shift in the process and the outcome.

I SHOULD HAVE BEEN A WEATHERMAN

Let's be very clear—the position of the meteorologist and the importance of her role in our lives is well respected and extremely necessary. However, in what other field can an individual be wrong and still remain respected? Definitely not in the field of educational administration.

To be a successful school administrator and ultimately the chief education officer of a school district, an individual must reach the conclusion that at no time will 100 percent of the individuals he represents completely agree with his decision. From board members to parents, to the students he serves, the surrounding community, and any other individual in the public who wants to chime in, for every person who is happy with a decision, several more aren't.

It is imperative that an administrator understand that this is the case before she signs on with a school or a district. Some leaders have a hard time accepting that individuals will go against their decisions, especially when they are made in the best interest of the students and the district. A school administrator must accept that she will be wrong 50 percent of the time. When the meteorologist calls for a chance of rain and the sun remains all day, the poor prediction is met with the gratitude that it was wrong, and the day was more pleasant.

Conversely, when no rain is predicted for the afternoon but a quick-moving dark storm cloud hovers over the ballfield and delays the little league championships, the mistake is categorized alongside the statement, "It's tough to predict the weather." Unlike the weatherman, constituents who are unhappy with an administrative decision will definitely make it known.

Thus, a true leader must be prepared to meet, accept, and respond in an amicable manner to all those stakeholders who disagree with the decision he made and is not favorable to their cause or conducive to their needs. Perfect example—the snow day.

YOU MAKE THE CALL!

Mary Jansen is a first-year superintendent preparing for her first Winter storm as a chief school administrator. As she anxiously waits and watches the weather report throughout the evening, she sets her alarm for 4 a.m. to ensure that she wakes in time to contact her plant engineer to see how snow removal is progressing around the district.

A little after 4 o'clock, Mary calls Joe Pepe, a twenty-five-year veteran in the district.

"Good morning. How's it looking, Joe?"

Joe replies, "Well, Ms. J., we were out here all night getting the lots cleaned and ready, but it looks like we may run out of salt if the temperature doesn't heat up a little bit."

"Oh, boy. Do you think we can still open, Joe?"

Joe shares the district's history with the new education leader.

"Well, I'm not sure. But I will tell you, Dr. Vargas never closed school."

At 4:15 a.m., Mary is faced with her first major dilemma as the district's new school chief.

What additional steps does Mary needs to consider to make the right decision?

Consider both scenarios (closing school or remaining open). What are some pros and cons stakeholder groups might have about the decision she must make?

COACHES' CORNER

1. The decision to close school unexpectedly due to an event or an emergency can be very difficult for educational leaders. How is this type of decision affected by local politics and involvement by different stakeholder groups?
2. Discuss an event or professional experience when a school closing occurred unexpectedly. What did the administration do well? What could it have done differently?
3. With a decision like this, half the members of the community will agree with the decision and half won't. As an administrator, how would you handle the criticism you will receive from those individuals not happy with your decision?

Chapter 2

The Decision-Making Process

Decision making is the most important process an educational leader will take part in during his tenure in the position. School district superintendents, building principals, administrators, and supervisors are responsible for making decisions that can have a significant impact on students, teachers, and the overall educational system. The decision-making process is critical in educational leadership as seemingly simple or obvious decisions can lead to very unexpected outcomes.

School leaders must consider the potential consequences of their decisions on the education system over time. In consideration of the local decisions that school administrators must make to keep a district moving forward and ensure that students are successful, a school leader must consider several important areas when making the best decisions for his school, district, or organization.

THE IMPACT ON STAKEHOLDERS

Decisions that educational leaders make affect various stakeholders. Students, teachers, parents, and members of the surrounding community are just several stakeholder groups where the decisions that school administrators make can impact the learning experience, influence morale, and affect relationships between the schools and the stakeholders within the community they serve.

It is extremely important that any school leader knows his stakeholder groups and the important individuals involved in each group. By understanding the pulse and the needs of each group and how these needs affect the support that each group lends to the school leader directly, he can ultimately use stakeholders to his advantage to gain support for a decision.

RESOURCE ALLOCATION

It is imperative that school leaders are aware of the funding available to them, especially when considering a new program or something that needs to occur in the school or district. The administrator does not want to involve stakeholders and outside groups in a process that will lend itself to making an impact on a district or organization, only to have the project or initiative halted for lack of funding.

LONG-TERM DECISIONS

Educational leaders make long-term decisions that can greatly impact the school community. As the administrator plans for changes based on curricular trends and mandates, personnel needs, financial constraints, and upgrades to facilities, many actions have long-lasting effects on the makeup of the educational landscape. The decisions the leader makes affect her long-term plans in the district, school, or organization.

UNINTENDED CONSEQUENCES

As this should always be a school leader's concern, some obvious decisions can lead to unfavorable outcomes due to unintended consequences. They occur when leaders lose sight of what is important to the educational system and let down their guard due to trust issues, outside influencers, or personal choice.

School administrators must work to identify potential outcomes of the decisions they make by asking stakeholders of the educational system to help identify any concerns and potential impact that may come from those decisions.

COMPLEX INTERACTIONS

Although usually not seen in this light, educational systems are extremely complex, with numerous interacting components that seemingly cross over on any given day. Most individuals view a school district only as a system that delivers educational instruction to students. In reality, school district operations include more business components than tenets of the field of education.

Yes, the vehicle to deliver instruction to students and the formula for a strong pedagogical foundation are the key mission of a board of education.

However, most districts have the largest overall budget and employ the greatest number of employees of any company or business in the city or township.

With this comes a greater responsibility for budget, financial stability, personnel resources, facilities oversight and upgrades, security, payroll, and even traffic safety and wellness. The school leader plays an extremely vast and diverse role in the functionality of the community she serves.

Simple decisions may interact with other factors in ways that leaders do not foresee. For example, changes to the grading system might impact student motivation or teacher behavior in unanticipated ways. Other decisions that the leader makes may have a tax impact on local citizens or cause changes to other programs or departments.

POLITICAL AND CULTURAL FACTORS

Educational decisions are often influenced by political considerations and cultural factors. What appears to be a straightforward choice may have political implications or face opposition from various interest groups, leading to unexpected resistance or consequences.

The educational leader must decide wisely when considering the choices she makes and how those choices will impact the students, their families, and the political atmosphere that surrounds the system itself. This especially holds true considering the cultural equity that must be met in each district, school, and associated organization. The administrator must ensure that decisions that are made affect each group in the same, positive manner, not make one group stand out or be spotlighted for any purpose.

ETHICAL AND EQUITY CONSIDERATIONS

Ethical and equity issues must always be at the forefront of decision making for educational leaders. Decisions that seem straightforward from logistical standpoints may have ethical implications related to fairness, inclusion, and social justice. Where equity is concerned, decisions are not only based on color, creed, and race but have implications related to individuals with disabilities and their access to programs and facilities.

Further, equity in its simplest form is ensuring that students from one part of town have the same as students from the other part of the district. Here, the school administrator cannot assume that all school sites are equal, and although transformational leadership includes providing an autonomous platform for teachers, inequity in studies among grade bands and schools can be detrimental to a leader gaining the support she needs from stakeholders.

Administrators must consider frequent equity audits to not only ensure that materials and supplies include the correct components for equitable distribution across the curriculum but also equity in access across the entire school community. If an audit presents inequities throughout the district, the administrator should act to add the materials, program, and so forth to the other sites instead of removing what already exists. This will avoid any animosity among sites, employees, and between other members of the administrative team.

DATA AND EVIDENCE

Any decisions the leader makes that lack a basis in research, data trends, or have not been vetted by stakeholders may lead to negative outcomes. Thus, each decision needs a range and direction of research and data to support it. Further, as it is very easy to control the narrative when reviewing data, the school administrator should consider presenting all sides of the story to control the narrative itself and ensure that stakeholders and others can review how the data is trending.

Using data to support decisions allows stakeholders to know that the decisions are backed by research and have been vetted by the school district professionals. Using the data appropriately to prove that the decision is the correct one for the school, district, or organization is an important part of the process.

ADAPTABILITY

An educational leader must gauge the adaptability of a decision to the surrounding educational environment. In other words, will the work and the potential outcomes from the decision be accessible and available to all stakeholder groups, or at least be able to adapt to the needs of each specific group?

It is important for the educational leader to understand that sustainable programs (programs that last over time) are most important when considering the success of his role as a leader in the district, school, or organization. No one wants to start a program or an initiative that he has worked hard on only to stop it the following year. Therefore, a decision that helps to create some part of the educational system must be designed so that it is adaptable to specific groups and can withstand future growth and challenges that the district may face.

The only way that the school administrator can ensure adaptability and sustainable longevity for any decision she makes is to understand the landscape before her. What are the potential downfalls and positive reactions that such a decision will have on the community? What does the near and distant future mission have that aligns with this current decision? Will she have stakeholder support when the current stakeholders change or are replaced?

Adaptability is arguably the most important characteristic in any role. Leaders must be adaptable not only to different situations that they face but they must adapt to the needs of those they lead. As those members in the leader's charge change through time, the leader must adapt and attenuate her style to accommodate the individual and collective needs of the members of the group. In decision making for school leaders, adaptability is even more pressing because the leadership role contains several moving parts based on the daily interactions the leader has among the stakeholders and other outside influencers.

SUSTAINABLE IMPROVEMENT

Educational leaders need to be adaptable and open to feedback loops. Even when decisions do not yield the expected outcomes, the ability to learn from these experiences and adjust future decisions is critical for ongoing improvement in educational leadership.

The improvement trends that an educational leader must seek need to lead to sustainable improvement. In educational leadership roles, leaders' decisions rely on actions in which the expectation is that the leader will enhance the district, school, or organization in a way that advances aptitude in a particular subject or other area of the educational system. Any plan of action surrounding such advancements must include steps to ensure that the intended outcomes are sustainable for an extended period. In other words, a leader doesn't want to show great improvement one year, then suffer a major loss over the next several years.

Sustainable improvement becomes realized when—and only when—the leader has strong buy-in from stakeholder groups, especially those groups directly related to the improvement at hand. In educational leadership, test score increases can only be sustainable if the improvement plans are supported by the teachers. For facilities restoration or building an athletic field, the sport teams and township recreation squads must have some say in what is being designed and an understanding of how it will affect their children and the future of the community.

Sustainable improvement doesn't always mean that the improvement will be immediate or enhanced at an alarming rate. Rather, however fast or slow the improvement "moves," it will be acceptable because the decisions has support from stakeholders and members of the community.

MORAL, ETHICAL, AND LEGAL (MEL) CONSIDERATIONS IN DECISION MAKING

Educational leaders are constantly making decisions that affect the future of their students, families, and the community they serve. What draws many individuals to a career in educational leadership is the opportunity to effect change in a system by constantly dealing with issues and making decisions based on the key pillars of the education landscape.

Although education and business are never considered synonymous, the reality is that running a district or a school is identical to running a company. In fact, most school districts, educational systems, and organizations are the largest employer in a community. A district most likely has the largest number of employees, the biggest budget, and arguably is in the business of producing and cultivating the most important widget—our children and the future leaders of tomorrow. With all these moving parts, the school leader must maintain the support of stakeholders and recognize influencers to ensure that he has support during and after he makes a decision.

Coming up with the answer is simple. It's the way the leader gets to the final decision that significantly impacts his standing in the educational system, grows (or shrinks) his political capital, and provides a level of support to ensure that his future decisions are supported among more stakeholders.

In every decision the school leader makes, she must address three important considerations before deciding what would ultimately work best for her and the stakeholders involved in the situation. First, though, she needs to take a breath.

Barring a physical emergency or safety issue that is actively occurring, no decision in educational leadership needs to be made immediately. From suspensions to curricular changes, to reprimands for employees, to choosing a food menu for the upcoming week, nothing in our immediate charge can't wait a day or two "for further discussion and investigation" before a final decision is rendered. Now, the administrator can do further research, call a colleague for advice, or continue to investigate to grasp a clearer picture of what occurred.

As that is established, the administrator can further vet the conditions of the decision and weigh all the pros and cons in addressing the MEL considerations surrounding each issue she faces.

Moral

This is the most difficult value to consider when making a decision that impacts the educational process of the school community or the office. The leader must ensure that his morals do not come into play when he makes a determination about the issue at hand.

Every individual has his own moral compass and his own set of values and morals that have been instilled in him since birth, and they continue to grow and "flex" over the years. In any public education setting, it is improper and most likely against local policy and statute for any teacher, administrator, or school employee to pass one's ideology on to others. Thus, checking the moral consideration one makes as a leader to satisfy the M includes the leader's ability to ensure that all avenues have been discussed and every perspective has been reviewed.

Most importantly, the decision itself cannot be made based on the moral aptitude of the leader alone. One person's morals are another person's stance against those same values. This type of debating is the foundation of democracy: we can each have a different value strand introduced to us since birth and cultivated over time and still give others the opportunity to stand up for what they may believe in and agree to debate the topic. Regardless of any outcome or any decision made, the school leader must follow the appropriate protocols to ensure that he remains neutral when deciding what is best for his students, faculty, and district.

This is the hardest piece of the MEL decision-making paradigm. The answer can't be found in a textbook or learned with on-the-job mentoring and professional development. Instead, the leader must look inward at his own moral compass and ensure that what the community needs and what is reflected in society prevails even if they don't match what he believes.

Ethical

Ethical considerations stem from a particular code or decree followed by school administrators, board members, and other staff members in the field of education. As is the same with other career areas, a code of ethics is designed and enacted by a governing body that oversees that the code is being followed to ensure that members are held to a higher set of standards as they deal with members of the public and when being compared to other careers.

In the case of educational administration, several states incorporate a code of ethics into state statute to establish a clear understanding for administrators to adhere to in making decisions concerning topics such as nepotism, conflicts of interest, and using one's office for personal or financial gain.

For example, in New Jersey the governor appoints a board of commissioners to accept, review, and assess penalties on complaints received by the public on the actions of school administrators. Known as the School Ethics Commission (SEC), commissioners not only hear cases on incidents but also provide opinions for administrators and board of education members to ensure that they follow the code of conduct established by the department of education and state legislators.

In following an ethical code established by a supporting, outside organization, school administrators are given direct parameters to observe when making a decision. Thus, unlike moral concerns, ethical considerations in decision making are black and white. A set of ethics is either followed or it isn't.

Legal

The final area of the MEL decision-making paradigm is legal. Similar to the ethical step in which leaders follow a specific code with parameters to actions in the leadership role, legal considerations when making decisions are already established by a law-making government entity. Although the decisions may be up for interpretation by individuals and legal counsel, the facts, findings, and conclusions are straightforward and established through the assistance of the legal system and based on due process.

School administrators should always check with a legal representative prior to making decisions that will affect or impact students, other stakeholder groups, and the district as a whole. This especially holds true in the field of educational administration because major case law, labor law, and other statutes among different states have previously been tried and tested with opinions and outcomes to help the leader make informed decisions.

ISSUE, RULE, APPLICATION, CONCLUSION (IRAC)[1]

Another way that educational leaders make important and informed decisions is through a method known as IRAC. Although most often used in law and law-related exercises, IRAC can be very beneficial to the school administrator for every decision that needs to be made that affects the educational system.

IRAC stands for the issue, rule, application, and conclusion of a legal analysis. This method was first used during World War II as a military training exercise created to teach recruits how they could solve problems on the battlefield. The method was used because the military needed to train soldiers, who were considered "green"—new to combat and with very limited aptitude for tactics—to make decisions in the field. In educational leadership, the method is used to identify, research, and draw conclusions to specific scenarios that affect the environment of the school system.

Each area of the IRAC template relates to the major themes of the school scenario itself. First, a synopsis of the problem at hand should include the facts of the case, an outline of what occurred, and whether a decision was made or relief granted. The method continues as follows:

Issue—Identify the issue(s) of the problem that the leader is trying to solve.

- The school leader must not assume that he has only one issue to address when making this decision. For each specific incident or decision, several parties or stakeholders may have relevant concerns that may affect the outcome.

Rule—List any state or federal statutes of law or district policies that may be relevant to the decision. Is there case law or has any previous decision been made in similar situations?

- Most often, school districts have policies to identify procedures, state statutes, and pertinent personnel related to nearly every decision that needs to be made in an educational system.

Application—The school leader must realize how the facts as outlined for the situation at hand intersect with the statutes, policies, and protocols of the educational system, and how each relates to the issues that the school leader has identified.

- The administrator must ensure that she recognizes how the district's policies and state and federal laws apply to the situation she faces before she makes a decision that will affect stakeholders. Without understanding how the application of the issue relates to what has already been established either by the local governing body or outside influences, she risks making a decision that not only will be incorrect but could have a negative impact on the district, school, or organization that she represents. This impact could be financial in nature and cost her political capital as well.

Conclusion—What are the possible outcomes based on the facts, issues, rules, and application realized? Further, was some conclusion already made; and if it was, what could have been done differently to ensure the most effective outcome should an issue of this nature happen again?

- Every decision will have an impact, and the impact will affect different groups in different ways. As the educational leader makes her decision based on the information provided and the research she has obtained, she must feel confident in her conclusion and her ultimate decision. However, she must also recognize that as an educational leader, there is always room for improvement, and it is most important to ensure that she continues to be consistent in making similar decisions in the future.

Although the IRAC method is an analysis that includes what seems to be a written reporting template, educational leaders should master the method and be able to analyze specific scenarios in this manner prior to making decisions. Just like MEL and other decision-making tools that a school leader uses to operate the district and schools effectively, it is important that the administrator knows how to provide such an analysis on a daily basis and for nearly every decision she makes that impacts the system.

YOU MAKE THE CALL!

Lou Nello has been the head of the football parent organization for the past six years. His oldest son graduated three years ago, and his other son, Franco, is a senior captain on the team and a Division I prospect. As the building principal, you have met Lou on several occasions and at the last two home games in which your team has beaten opponents by at least three touchdowns.

Lou asked to meet with you after Friday's game, and you set a time on Monday morning to see him in your office. During the meeting, Lou began to discuss how important this year is to his son and that several scouts have been seen at both home and away games over the past several weeks. With only three weeks left in the season, Lou is hoping that his son's performance earns him a full scholarship to one of the schools on the East Coast.

Lou went on to explain that he knows the superintendent very well and that he graduated and played football on the same team with two of the board members, who feel that you have what it takes to be the next superintendent of the district. He appreciated the time you gave him for the meeting and had only one request. Lou explained that because the last several games had large score differences, the head coach had put in most of the second-string players in the last quarter of the game to not embarrass the players on the visiting team.

Unfortunately, this caused Lou's son not to play, and sitting out hurts his exposure with scouts, even though his being on the field would absolutely look like your team was being unsportsmanlike with such a point spread. Lou basically doesn't care about how the "other" team feels and wants his son to play as much as possible. The last three games of Franco's career in the district are coming up, and the opposing teams are the weakest ones that the school has played all season.

Lou would like you to discuss this with the coach.

Discuss some of the implications that this conversation and expected outcome have on your role as a school administrator.

What would your next steps be?

What other individuals would you discuss this with, and what would you say to Lou?

COACHES' CORNER

1. Describe a local decision like this that a school administrator made. What were some issues he/she faced with making the decision?
2. Use the MEL paradigm to go through the decision-making process for this situation.
3. What are the political concerns with any decision that you make in this case as the principal?

ENDNOTE

[1] Touro Law Center. (2006).

Chapter 3

Influencing Matters

The power of influencing others can be described as one of the most important tenets of educational leadership in the twenty-first century. Influencing others includes understanding the question, need, or problem at hand and the definition of the different types of individual personalities that a school leader will face within an educational setting.

Influencing matters. For an educational leader to ensure that the appropriate decisions are made for a district, school, or the organization, she must successfully influence the local political decision-making process. This influence may include her board, local government elected and appointed officials, and all other stakeholders who have a vested interest in the day-to-day and long-term planning that may affect the community as a whole.

Each school administrator builds a specific toolbox to ensure that he has the correct set of tools to exert influence on others. The tools used are based on how an administrator has been trained, who has trained him, and where the tool will be used in connection with the decisions needed to be made.

Although a toolbox of this nature most always contains many of the standard tools for every school leader, each administrator's box also is filled with a style and the methods that he is most comfortable using when he is attempting to influence others to support his decisions. This may include a specific method of delivery or an order of calling constituents to gain support for the decision he intends to make. Other tools include using feedback loops, performing a SWOT (strengths, weaknesses, opportunities, threats) analysis, evaluating options, and reviewing forecasts and projected outcomes.

Regardless of the tools at his discretion, the leader will only be successful in influencing others in supporting his decisions if he understands who the other influencers are who will either agree with or dispute his decision. Sometimes, these influencers are not people but policies and procedures that influence decisions based on a set of conditions. It is important for the leader to wholly understand that many of these outside influencers are competing with him to create a separate path for a different solution or decision.

Take the example of calling a snow day. From the start, even before the school administrator has made his decision, a percentage of stakeholders already disagree with the decision he intends to make. This happens because individuals have different thoughts, experiences, or maybe just enjoy going against the status quo. Regardless, the leader must quickly pinpoint which influencers will be most affected and by how much. Not all influencer groups will be affected by every local decision; however, recognizing which stakeholder and constituent groups attempt to influence the leader and other educational personnel will provide the leader with the insight and reflection necessary to be prepared to inform all those involved why the final decision was made.

Chart 3.1 outlines the four levels of influence of educational personnel and where the influencers fall when considering the placement of these influences relative to the personnel making the decisions. The farther away the influencers are situated from the targeted administrator, the less value they hold when local decisions are made that impact local stakeholders.

LEVEL 1 INFLUENCERS

Level 1 influencers include considerations for decisions to be based on a set of morals, cultural conditioning, or familial obligations that can affect the operations of the school or the district as a whole. Level 1 influencers are the closest to the decision-making process for two reasons.

First, the influencers at Level 1 always relate to the needs of the students, faculty, and staff and the concerns of the family. Going back to the snow day example, the leader must first consider the conditions for students getting to and from school and the ability of parents and guardians to ensure appropriate pickup as part of his decision. Conversely, will keeping students home during a snow event be impossible or a burden to most parents in the community?

Level 1 influencers may include the culture of the community during such an event. Does the city or town historically clear roads and salt them in an appropriate manner or wait until the event has almost concluded so as not to put a financial burden on the taxpayers or true physical harm to the roadways if accumulation is too light? Or does the district have a long-standing tradition of closing during the first snowfall so everyone can ski at the local mountain?

Second, the morals and family needs that arise from this level of stakeholder influence are completely different for every stakeholder in the school,

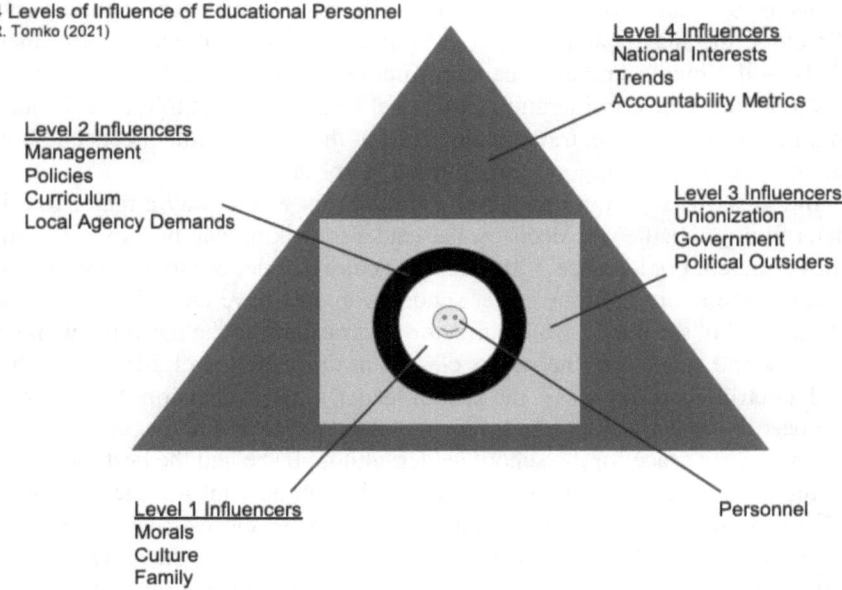

Figure 3.1 Levels of Influence of Educational Personnel. Tomko, R.D. (2021). Navigating the workplace: What school executives should know about labor relations.

district, or organization. In other words, the needs of one family in consideration of a possible decision will never completely mirror the needs of another family who lives in another part of the city or township. Further, one family's moral compass and what the core unit values most likely will never match all members of the school community. Consequently, it is extremely important that the school leader keeps his personal morals, cultural, and familial values out of the decision-making process because, as the educational leader, he is "speaking" for those families and stakeholders he serves.

The school leader must sort through the varying concerns that Level 1 influencers place on each and every decision that affects the school system and how his decision, in turn, may establish a burden for some stakeholders and a benefit for others. Although it can be a complex task for even a seasoned school administrator, it is very attainable if the leader takes a transparent approach, remains consistent, and understands the political landscape.

LEVEL 2 INFLUENCERS

Level 2 influencers include management positions (administrators the leader may report to, elected and appointed officials), policies, curriculum, and the demands of local government agencies such as town managers, public works directors, the mayor and committee/council members, as well as fire marshals, police chiefs, and the local construction official. Once the school leader acknowledges the considerations for Level 1 and makes an initial decision, it is time for her to concentrate on the needs of the Level 2 influencers and how she may be able to support them in making her decision.

In the snow day example, Level 2 influencers would play a major role in determining whether the decision the leader is making can be supported and substantiated. For instance, if the school's chief decides not to call a snow day because too many families in her school wouldn't have enough time to find child care but the public works director informs her that he has three workers out sick and cannot get the streets cleared in time, the Level 2 influencer has had a detrimental impact on the school leader's initial decision. However, in the best interest of safety, the leader will need to close schools.

The saving grace for the school leader: although she had the best intentions of the needs of her stakeholders in mind, she can now inform the stakeholders—who will be very upset with her decision to close—that she had no choice due to the absenteeism at one municipal department that plays a major part in providing safe travel to and from schools during a snow event.

LEVEL 3 INFLUENCERS

At Level 3 is a broader set of individuals who may look to influence local decisions that the school leader needs to make. As many district schools across the country are unionized, an administrator's decision can always potentially impact faculty and staff. Thus, the school leader must consider how the decisions he makes will affect the morale and performance of his workforce.

In any situation, the potential impact on the district labor force and its representation does not necessarily mean that each decision must follow the demands as set forth by those individuals. Rather, a good school leader knows to keep the labor leadership involved in the decision-making process and well informed whenever a decision has been made. Again, leaders may disagree on this point; however, at least the school administrator has made an informed decision and would have his chance to explain his reasoning.

Other Level 3 influencers who must be considered include government offices and political outsiders. This includes a district or community's extended political universe, such as state senators, assembly officials, and elected delegates of county government. Most school leaders' day-to-day decisions that affect the educational system will not cause extended government outsiders to become involved. Except for photo opportunities, ribbon-cutting ceremonies, or special visits from other dignitaries, outside influence is very scarce.

Most often, the school leader can use the mission and actions of these outside Level 3 influencers to help sway a decision and curry favor with local constituent groups. In the snow day example, if the governor calls a state of emergency based on the predicted fallout from an impending storm, administrators can use that action when measuring the pros and cons for closing school for the day. The same concept holds true for bills, statutes, and laws established by the legislature and carried out by the state education commissioner that may be "unpopular" based on the local politics of the city or township the school leader serves. In other words, the local political barometer may not support the tenets of a law that has been newly adopted, but the administrator can easily turn to the elected legislative body for blame on its implementation.

LEVEL 4 INFLUENCERS

As shown in chart 3.1, the broadest scope of influence over school leader personnel includes entities that have interests on a national scale, certain trends in education and across the country, as well as established measures of success to hold education systems accountable.

National interests change rapidly with the flow of information and viewpoints established by media outlets, actions around the world, and a response to specific events that occur across the nation. Politically speaking, Level 4 influencers create the most "friction" for school leaders when dealing with programs, policies, and personnel throughout the organization. As these influencer needs trickle down to the other levels, school leaders must keep abreast of the issues at hand to be prepared if and when they affect the local decision-making process.

School systems often see this occur when worldwide events lead to an aggressive pro- or anti- statement made by students and staff members about a particular action. During the 2023 Israel–Hamas war, wavering support and the lengthy campaign led to radical shifts in support for original efforts to suppress attacks. This then caused the worldly viewpoints to trickle down to lower-level influencers who were somewhat forced to take sides as constituents rallied around the daily events portrayed through the media and reported around the world.

Soon after, local (Level 1) stakeholders who were taken aback by the shift in the paradigm of the original campaign and may have had family or friends affected brought the conflict to their communities and school systems, looking to hold rallies and pass resolutions supporting or admonishing government actions. As emotions became supercharged, school leaders needed to work hard to ensure that their own morals did not impact students' rights or disrupt the educational process.

For some, this issue (the same as other nationally charged issues in the past such as Black Lives Matter) became difficult to navigate as local political influencers and elected officials began to show support for sides to enjoy political favor during a quick election cycle. School leaders needed to remain confident in their policies, procedures, and the laws that govern First Amendment rights and how those laws pertain to students and school employees.

Administrators who are continuously successful when these issues arise understand early on the potential for outside influencers (Level 4) to quickly make their way to the local level. They are overly prepared for the incoming climate and review the school system's legal responsibilities and student/employee rights with legal counsel prior to an event occurring. A successful school leader would also reach out to Level 2 influencers (police chief, mayor, etc.) prior to it reaching their level so that the local government leadership can be on the same page when handling a situation of this magnitude with the potential to have a lingering effect on the leader, her district or school, and the community as a whole.

Along with national trends and reactions to matters on a worldly scale, Level 4 influencers can also surface as educational trends that are sweeping across the United States. Although it is very unusual to have this occur because different regions of the country have different needs, a national push from the White House, Congress, or a global entity usually brings with it a sweeping overhaul of a facet of the education system.

An example of this was the No Child Left Behind Act (NCLB), which attempted to put in place federal monies and programs to help ensure that all children were receiving the same free and appropriate education across the country. A major consideration of the act was that all children, by a certain time, would score 100 percent on their state's standardized test. This is a formidable goal and one that politically had to be supported by nearly all members of Congress. How could any member of Congress not think that we could provide a system where all students would earn a perfect standardized score? The fact is that that goal was never attainable.

There is no way that every individual will perform perfectly on a standardized assessment. The fact is that different communities in different states and regions have different socioeconomic makeups and hurdles that students and families must attend to. This no longer includes discussions only about poor school systems with high rates of poverty. In fact, seemingly more factors come to the forefront in considering how schools can be affected. These include technology deficits, government funding formulas, bullying, gender bias, teacher preparation, and violence in schools.

Tied into these trends are accountability metrics that put the onus on schools to ensure that students perform well to compare one local community to the next. Talk about a politically charged atmosphere? Standardized scores based on accountability assessments are marred by many of those factors mentioned in the previous paragraph. Although they only measure the aggregate of the school population and do not always take specific factors into consideration in striking the accountability formula, these Level 4 influencers are tied into the worth of a community, home values, and ignite the politically charged conversations that sometimes allow Level 1 influencers and community stakeholders to point the proverbial finger instead of focusing on the positive metrics that a school system delivers.

PUTTING IT ALL TOGETHER

Understanding the levels of influence that a school leader inherits will truly help her make appropriate decisions for her school or district through her awareness of what may be coming her way. To truly see how the levels dictate how influencing others matters in the process, gun control provides a concrete example of how all four influencer levels can impact local decision making.

In 2023 alone, 346 school shooting incidents were reported across the United States,[1] the highest total on record since 1966.[2] School shootings have been a nationally recognized issue since the Columbine incident in April 1999. At that time, parents and citizens across the country realized that events of this nature don't only occur in violent, urban neighborhoods and that every student and community is susceptible to this form of violence at any time.

As shootings have become more prevalent in school settings and unimaginable student and staff casualties have amassed over the past two decades, more training protocols have been put in place to help stop an event from occurring and more so to mitigate the potential loss of life after a school shooting occurs. Outrage and outcry from community groups and legislators unfortunately are short-lived. Rather, the strike while the iron is hot mentality usually comes into play, and the pressure to mandate changes in gun control laws and school safety ebbs and flows as new nationwide issues come to light and strong lobbies work to change the narrative.

What happens in this case is that instead of waiting for sweeping change and financial support on a national scale to deal with what most arguably is an epidemic, individual school leaders work to ensure that their schools, district offices, students, and employees are safe daily. Without many parameters in place, school systems employ security officers, design and construct lockdown and evacuation procedures, purchase protective products and surveillance systems, and work with local authorities to ensure that there is coordination among school leadership, police, and fire in case an emergency occurs.

A Level 4 influence, such as school shootings, evidenced on such a national scale must cause a school administrator to take immediate and ongoing steps when preparing for the inevitable impact it will have on the closer level influencers in his community. In such an example, the response by government officials will be politically charged and create challenges for any school leader who intends to join in a national or even statewide debate. Rather, a school leader should tend closely to the Level 1 and Level 2 influencers and the needs of his own students and staff members to ensure that her stakeholders know that she has their best interests and safety in mind—at all times.

YOU MAKE THE CALL!

As the new principal of Central Middle School, you have been charged with helping to bridge the cultural gap that has been widening at the school over the past five years. You have decided that while the weather is still warm, you will host a multicultural event called World Central Fusion to celebrate all the diverse backgrounds of the students and families in the middle school.

As you begin to plan the event, and after receiving approval from the school superintendent, you realize that this is a larger undertaking than you first imagined. You know it's the first time an event like this has ever been held at the school, and because it is your first big event as principal, you need it to be a success. One of your biggest concerns is that you will forget a represented culture or an important member of the school community due to your lack of experience in running an event this large.

What are your next steps? What will you do to include all the stakeholders from the school and the district?

COACHES' CORNER

1. How would you include influencers (as outlined in 3.1) in an event such as the one in the aforementioned scenario?

2. What are some concerns you may have in consideration of the political landscape of the educational system and some of the influencers who may be involved in the event?
3. How do you ensure that the stakeholders in the district don't view your decision to hold a program of this magnitude so soon after your arrival at the school as a political move on your part?

ENDNOTES

[1] K–12 School Shooting Database. www.k12ssdb.org.
[2] Wolf, C. (2024). School Shootings by State. *U.S. News and World Report.*

Chapter 4

Avoiding the Political Tsunami

Along with the multitude of decisions school administrators make every day that have a positive impact on a school district and its stakeholders, a school leader can also make decisions leading to a string of events that can cause irreparable damage to the school chief's career and the district itself. Quick, emotional, and rash decisions can cause great political harm to educational leaders and administrators who believe they understand more than they do.

As a school administrator rises through different leadership roles, he is faced with making decisions related to his position. While a superintendent of schools will handle systemic concerns at the local, state, and federal political levels, a building level leader will deal with the day-to-day influences of stakeholder groups closely aligned with the students, faculty, and staff. Meanwhile, he needs to monitor an entire separate political structure dealing with the internal employee-employer relations, employee-employee conflicts, working with a union, and the power struggle between administration and staff.

Navigating politics is not easy. Most experts would argue that it's a learned trait, and the most successful individuals understand that you win some and you lose some. An experienced, sound school leader first understands that the environment is politically charged, although most outside individuals won't see it because children are involved. Simply stated, educational leaders who can fill a résumé with career stops that include lengthy tenures understand one thing about the position . . . to be careful not be political but to be very politically savvy.

Along with understanding that only 50 percent of an educational leader's constituent base will agree with a decision she has made 50 percent of the time, a strong leader also knows how to wade through the local political waterways to get what she needs for her district, students, and staff while ensuring that her own initiatives and goals are attainable and can sustain a positive, progressive growth pattern while she is in the post.

Being politically savvy provides her with a shield of sorts to thwart any misconceived notions from others that her decisions are based on the needs of a political machine, a political platform, or a specific individual looking to curry favor in support of an individual agenda. Instead, understanding the local and surrounding politics and how to prepare for and handle such issues is key to any leader's overall success in the position. This can be accomplished in several key ways.

LEARN THE HISTORICAL LANDSCAPE

A school leader must involve herself in every aspect of the school and local community. From academic evenings to extracurricular shows and recreation softball games, to community events, becoming part of the district, township, or city is the only way that stakeholders will truly believe their school leader has a vested interest in the success of the district or school itself. As a side note, the minute a school leader doesn't feel vested in the interests of the school district or community is the time for her to start looking for another job.

Along with the importance of fully immersing himself in the community, the leader must do his part to study the historical political landscape of the district itself. Besides understanding the current powerbrokers, it is extremely important to know who the key political players were in the past and how they are still involved in or connected to the schools. What are some major past projects or programs that were successful? Which ones failed? More importantly, why did they fail?

History is an extremely important guide to carving a future path. Without a leader knowing what once worked—or didn't work—in the district and community, he cannot create a strategic plan and goal set to move the needle forward. However, as a cautionary tale, learning and engaging in the historical landscape of a school system doesn't necessitate aligning oneself with all the past players who resurface at some point in your tenure. It's important for a school administrator to meet with and be cordial to all the past players within the political arena, but it is also important to tread lightly until the administrator fully understands who his allies are or what any ask may cost him in the future.

MUTUAL RESPECT

It seems like a simple concept, but mutual respect is one of the most important characteristics a school leader can have to be successful and considered competent in his post. On any given day, tensions can (and will) flare up with at least one member of a stakeholder group. Whether it's a student who receives a reprimand, a parent who is unhappy with a decision or action by the administration or a staff member, a teacher or other district employee who is upset with any number of things that can affect the educational environment, or a citizen who is not happy with her tax bill or students who walk on her lawn on the way home from school, it is a safe bet that a heated conversation is somewhere in the making.

At times, disagreements and ill feelings may come from political stakeholders—town council members, a local mayor or assembly official, or your own board of education trustee. Regardless of who it is and whether you perceive them to be wrong, a successful servant leader must ensure that he upholds a level of mutual respect so that he remains in control of the situation at hand.

To ensure that this occurs, the leader should restate the aggressors' concerns and offer that she understands the issue at hand. An appropriate follow-up question or two, which seemingly can be answered by the other individual, also shows that the leader holds a level of respect high enough for the other person in that he is wholly invested in their concerns.

Above all, the leader must continually control the conversation so that it does not become an argument or yelling at one another. To ensure that this occurs, the administrator cannot take the confrontation personally, realizing that she is there only to run the district, school, or organization well. Regardless of the outcome, remaining consistent by following the policies and procedures of the school district in an equitable fashion keeps politics out of the process.

IDENTIFY A STRONG ALLY

When a school administrator first enters a district or organization, she most likely has little human and political capital in her arsenal. What she does have is her reputation, the commitment she has made to her new home, and the overwhelming ability to follow all the necessary rules of educational administrative engagement when first stepping into a new position.

After learning the local, political, and educational landscape through listening and initiating feedback/feedforward loops, the school leader should work to carefully cultivate a set of allies to help her navigate any hurdles that she will face during her transition, assist her in understanding the questions that will arise, and pinpoint the relationships she needs to make to solidify her footprint in the organization.

To reiterate, this must be a politically savvy consideration, not a political one. Surrounding yourself with friends and confidants who embrace your mission and goals for the betterment of the district, school, or department is the best way to lead your planning and grow your success. The alliance must be made so as not to set your confidants apart from others; rather, any new ally should be seen as being on a parallel level with others in your organization where only a few know that he is the gateway to your ear.

DON'T SPEAK... LISTEN

The best advice given to me as a new young administrator back when the average age of school leaders was fifty was to "keep your mouth shut!" Today, the advice is softened and explained a little more; it is better most times to listen to your constituents rather than always telling them what to do. Further, in any situation, but especially in education, it is extremely imperative that a school leader questions before he comments. This seems easy to remember, but somehow it is very difficult for leaders to live by.

The reason leaders don't always follow this credo is simple: they know they are the leaders. At times, individuals in charge of a district, school, or organization feel obligated—or prompted—to always have an answer, always have a path to success, and always have what it takes to get to the next step in a process. Unfortunately, this is not the case.

Regardless of a school administrator's level of aptitude in consideration of a specific situation that has occurred or something planned to take place, someone always can assist the leader to ensure that the outcome surpasses any expected level of success. In other words, school administrators don't know it all even though many times they act like they do.

You do no harm in requesting assistance for specific initiatives or ideas from constituents, consultants, or seasoned colleagues who may have experience with an issue or an upcoming project you are about to engage in with the organization. One example would be a referendum construction project.

Many school communities at some point will charge the sitting school chief with designing and marketing a school building project to deal with expanding enrollment, outdated infrastructure, or aging facilities. Although through his board and architect the school leader will have an idea of what the project scope will entail, the needs of the community must come from the community stakeholders themselves. Although this seems like a natural step in the process, many nuances must be considered prior to bringing a project of this magnitude to the public.

This is where listening—to those stakeholder groups and other school leaders who have been involved with multiple building projects—is most important. It ensures that the leader doesn't get to the end of the project and find out she missed something or should have spoken with other experts in the field who had already been through something of this magnitude.

It is important to listen as much as possible to any and every informed source prior to making any decisions that the school leader will regret. The more research-based evidence that a leader can be afforded prior to making a decision or formulating a plan will be most beneficial to her success in the long run.

ALWAYS INFORM

A school leader can only avoid a devastating political situation if he consistently informs his constituents about the situation at hand. As this isn't always possible in a political atmosphere, the more aware that the administrator can be when considering the political atmosphere that will attach itself to a local issue, the more prepared he will be to escape the fallout unharmed.

The term transparency is used skillfully by seasoned school leaders to bring awareness to their administration and its ability to work out in the open and to make important decisions that affect students and the community with the input and reliance on the wants and needs of the stakeholders. However, saying the word and living its meaning are two completely different things.

Informing the base about upcoming decisions, changes, or programs that may have a lasting impact on the individuals that the leader serves is the only true way to avoid potential retribution. Does he know that a vote to lower the tax levy for the proposed budget will greatly harm the district in the future? Well, he better make sure he tells everyone that during a public meeting before the decision is made. Will removing teacher positions and programs affect test scores at certain grade levels? If so, that's not a comment to make after the scores are made public, but before those decisions will impact the future testing of his students.

The more informational and transparent the leader can be in all areas under his control, the better equipped he is to fend off the inevitable fallout he may face in the leadership role. Any educational leader who doesn't think that he may be faced with major political fallout isn't ready to lead. It doesn't have to be a decision that the leader himself makes. It can be decisions and mission of others in the community or even a response to an event completely out of his hands.

The COVID-19 pandemic taught the educational administration field that keeping constituents and stakeholders informed was the number two priority in leadership, directly behind school safety. After the health concerns of the outbreak had been somewhat controlled and the world was returning to some resemblance of a new normal, school leaders were faced with the difficult challenge to follow the rules that governed the country while being the proverbial punching bag for parents and other stakeholder groups who were completely against the state mandates that governed the schools.

As many superintendents and key district officials either retired after those pandemic years or were ousted by angry community groups who ran for spots on local boards of education, those school chiefs who were successful through their COVID-19 tenure did so by keeping all stakeholders informed of not only what protocols were established but who had established them and why. Those successful leaders also pinpointed the most vocal constituents and reached out to them to inform them directly about the protocols established through different agencies and others that were decided locally. This information highway educated the most boisterous and tight-knit political groups; the information led them to not agree but at least understand that certain things couldn't occur.

FEEDBACK/FEEDFORWARD LOOPS

A political impact cannot be identified without feedback loops. Besides allies that the leader herself has ascertained during her tenure in the district, acquiring feedback from stakeholder groups and individuals close to specific topics or concerns is the only way to fully gauge which crises may come and which can still be averted.

A school administrator can acquire feedback from different stakeholders formally or informally. The process can be as complex as holding a well-advertised meeting that includes a forum for the entire community at a school auditorium or as informal as asking her elementary principal to talk to parents outside at pickup and take a pulse on a specific topic, concern, or a decision that may affect or is affecting a school community.

Using feedback to make informed decisions and stay transparent is integral to being able to avoid the political tsunami that may come the leader's way if she is unaware of a situation that has brewed to an uncontrollable level. It is also important that the leader use these loops to check the temperature of her cabinet, knowing that she has a completely different landscape to manicure there.

Feedforward is not a term used as often as it should be in leadership circles, especially to curb any political movements established to negatively impact a leader in her leadership role. Feedforward provides the leader with the opportunity to take the feedback she has gained from her stakeholder groups and provide those same groups with upcoming solutions to help focus on a more productive future.

As the leader provides updates to all stakeholders through social media, public meetings, newsletters, and the like, she uses feedforward to cut off any upcoming political swell by diffusing a concern she received from the feedback she obtained in those sessions. Letting community members know that she is engaged in finding a solution to a current issue that may not have reared its head yet lets others know that she is in tune with happenings around the school or district and allows her to get ahead of the issue before it is formally announced by some other political means.

RESEARCH/EVIDENCE-BASED DECISIONS AND RESPONSES

Whenever possible, school administrators and educational leaders should use research-based evidence to make decisions and respond to requests or concerns by stakeholder groups. This is especially important when the leader is putting forth a new product, curriculum, or course design that may necessitate a formal vote with support from parents, faculty, and staff. Even specific vendors and consultants must be vetted to ensure that any background information or past work cannot be connected to some unexpected political tie. Remember, it is important to know who the players are prior to bringing someone to the forefront.

Gauging political savviness against being political will always weigh heavily on what the perception of others is and based solely on political gain. Evidence helps to level that concern when the leader can prove that the candidate or firm is best suited to get the job done in the most timely, cost-effective manner.

AVOID THE LOCAL TEA

Many school leaders get caught in and enjoy listening to the gossip that engulfs the school hallways, office backrooms, and the aisles of the local supermarket. A leader who fully involves himself in the local gossip dealings and rumor mills will one day end up in a political nightmare.

Nothing good can stem professionally from taking part in the happenings, relationships, personal occurrences, and legal matters of the members of the school and surrounding community. Yes, one can argue that to be successful in preparing for what may come across a leader's desk, knowing firsthand what certain key players in the community are experiencing is extremely important. However, knowing or engaging in conversations about these happenings are two completely different things.

As mentioned earlier, knowing the entire layout of the political landscape in a community is extremely valuable in ensuring that the educational leader has a successful tenure in the district, school, or organization. But responding to, agreeing with, or refuting personal, professional, or even political gossip places the leader directly in line with the politics surrounding the discussion. No longer does the leader stay outside the situation looking inward.

Rather, those leaders who fully engage in the back-and-forth tales that surround the district and other community leaders only find themselves tied into the political struggle and lose the upper hand when trying to defend a position or shed their own involvement with the individuals in question.

HOLD ON TIGHT

At some point in her career, a school administrator will make a horrific mistake. Besides taking full responsibility for her actions and apologizing to those involved with the promise to make changes to right the wrong, there's only one thing more to do . . . hold on tight.

School administrators and organizational leaders alike constantly make situations worse for themselves by continuing to defend what's just not defendable. And that is defending against perception.

Regardless of what has occurred or what a school leader has done to rectify the situation at hand, what others perceive had occurred or how the situation could have been handled can never be attenuated by the administrator himself. In other words, after a mistake and an inevitable mea culpa, nothing else that you say or do immediately afterward to try to excuse your actions will make a difference.

To get through any actions that may have a negative effect on the leader's charge, he must pause and avoid anything and everything that can continue the feeding frenzy that comes with something harmful that has occurred. This especially holds true with social media and an individual's need to read the community and parent blogs that constantly critique the decisions of school officials and leaders of a community. By responding to those posts or perpetuating discussions surrounding who's right or who's wrong, the issue stays at the forefront.

In leadership, and more specifically in education, news only lasts as long as the next newsreel. And in the world of education, the reel changes rapidly.

YOU MAKE THE CALL!

Anthony Varner is the newest member of the administrator's unit and a supervisor in the Cozy Meadows Public School District. Early in the year, Mr. Varner was put in charge of publications and made the decision that as sales were down, the district would benefit from moving away from a physical printed yearbook and instead, look to partner with a company that would supply digital yearbooks to students at half the cost.

During a spring meeting, the head of the parent-teacher organization contacted the main office and inquired about yearbook orders for the school year. The president was afraid that she may have missed an email that included the order form, and her son was looking forward to having his friends sign his book during Senior Signing Day, a tradition at the school since the early 1980s.

When the school principal received the president's message, she, too, was taken aback by the fact that she hadn't seen or heard much about yearbook sales throughout the school year. She immediately contacted Mr. Varner and asked for an update.

What possible issues stem from this scenario? What would be your next move if you were Mr. Varner?

COACHES' CORNER

1. What political implications will/may stem from the decision that Mr. Varner made?
2. What should Mr. Varner have done differently?
3. If you were advising Mr. Varner, what should his next steps be? What kind of damage control does he have to do to build support at the school or in the district?

Chapter 5

Navigating Local Politics

A successful educational leader knows how and when to be politically savvy. It is imperative that she be well-versed in the political landscape of the educational organization and how each political area influences the next.

Although it takes time to fully understand and grasp a historical context of the political layout of the community at large and, more directly, the school system, a prepared school leader understands that the navigation begins even before she first steps into the new position. Along with using her leadership skills to pinpoint the areas she may need to address and her ability to listen to her stakeholders before making any changes, her knowledge of influencers and the educational needs of the community will add value to how she is perceived.

An administrator knows that to have the support and the ability to make the decisions he needs for his school or district to progress means that he needs to dissect the individual needs of those individuals and groups who have a stake in the success of the system and those individuals who are most affected by its outcomes.

To do this, he must sharpen his savviness and stay away from entering the true political arena, performing favors, or making promises that he cannot keep or will compromise his position and career. It is very easy for a school leader to fall into such a trap because it is difficult for many individuals to firmly reply "no" without coming across as disrespectful, rude, or uninterested.

To this end, a respected school leader is one who can listen to the need or the request at hand; dissect what is asked and relate it to what is best for the district, school, or community; analyze its potential impact on the school system; and know before any decision is made what the political fallout will be once it is announced.

Being as savvy as she is, the school administrator also understands that she needs to use local political cues to her own career advantage, solidifying her position in the community and increasing her political capital based on her ability to navigate the decision to have the greatest effect, significance, and influence over all the important groups involved in the organization.

Understanding each group and its possible reaction to her decision is essential to moving forward in her role and is even more important for any future decisions that may impact the same stakeholder groups with a similar outcome. In other words, the more successful the school leader is in ensuring that certain members of the school community are amenable to her decision, the more support and trust she will garner from these groups, making future decisions easier to consider.

Conversely, poor decisions, especially ones perceived to negatively impact the same groups on multiple occasions, nearly always create a tense situation. Regardless of the school leader's track record in supporting certain specific entities, a harsh spotlight may shine on her office for an unspecified period. In these cases, it is crucial that the leader recognize which groups have been most affected by some of her decisions and why has she decided against them so often. Just as when one deals with his own children, it is important to say "yes" sometimes, even if it may be unpopular.

Moving forward in identifying ways to understand and handle a particular group of constituents, the school administrator must recognize that each group has a different expectation and must be approached in a different way.

THE TERM IS: MYOPIC

Most members of a school system are nearsighted about their own issues. Unless the school leader provides the constituent or stakeholder group with an outline of how a decision will affect all the moving parts of the school community, most often a myopic tone is established when fighting for position control over an issue.

A teacher teaches class three periods in a row and now has a break in which she can check her text messages. Her significant other tells her that he was at the dentist, and the office didn't have their dental card on file. He needs to provide a copy of it the next time either of them has a visit.

Frantic, the teacher realizes that she doesn't have a dental card either, and she must not have received it from the human resources department. She calls the human resources officer during lunch, but no one answers. She decides to stop by the HR office directly after work to ensure that she can get the card immediately.

At the human resources department, the teacher explains that she never received her dental card and that she tried to call during her lunch break, but no one answered. The receptionist takes her information and tells the teacher that HR will work on a replacement card and get back to her as soon as possible.

The next day the teacher is taken aback by the fact that she hasn't received a follow-up call or a message stating that her new dental card is ready to pick up. She decides to send a follow-up email, notifying the office that this is the second request she has made and that she needs the card to avoid being charged the full fee.

The teacher is establishing a myopic view of the situation and the response that she is getting from the human resources department. It's not her fault; rather, it is the most pressing issue on her mind at the moment, and she cannot conceptualize the plethora of work that the human resources department is prioritizing at the moment. Further, she can't imagine that when she is free during her lunch period, anyone else could be taking lunch at the same time.

In nearly every instance where a decision must be made, a school leader is faced with deciding with or against an individual or group with some myopic sense of what should occur. One can argue that most individuals can't—or won't—understand why a decision took so long to make in the first place.

To combat such a narrow sense of what possibly may occur, a school leader must get around this issue by stating some of his concerns and considerations directly from the outset. "I understand your questions, Ms. Jones . . . let me review the school board policies that pertain to this situation and whether other past projects have needed similar considerations."

Here, the school leader made it very clear that the ask was understood, but several other related areas may influence the decision or the process that will need to be followed. If the initial response had been different ("Ms. Jones, I don't think that's possible right now") and given without any explanation as to why a decision may be made, it would be extremely difficult for the school leader to backpedal and state that he needed to make specific considerations to come to the decision he made. Simply put, he looks as if he is not telling the truth, and he made the decision first based on impulse (or politics) and added the process later to escape any scrutiny from peers, the board, and the community at large.

WORKING WITH PARENTS

As parents are also understandably nearsighted most times, working with them is an extremely important skill that a school administrator must perfect to lead successfully in a school building or district. Consider the different layers of parental involvement and different types of parents.

The parental layers can be easily dissected. From the parent who is barely noticeable, participates when appropriate, and supports the facilitation that occurs by the teachers and educational staff in the buildings to the parent who constantly questions every move the district team makes, parental involvement changes from one year to the next.

Arguably, the level of involved parenting is the most difficult metric to predict in any educational setting. As more advocates and rights organizations come to the forefront with the mission to engage in as many educational organizations as possible to influence change in local schools, the more parents feel empowered to know more than the educational experts who are leading the educational system in the community.

Along with a layered parental engagement model, school leaders must also learn to identify and handle different types of parents.

PARENTS WHO THREATEN

These are the parents who attempt to persuade you to make an informed decision based on mostly idle threats of calling the superintendent (or board member), informing the news, or calling an attorney. Threatening parents are the easiest category to work with as long as the administrator stays calm and consistent while encouraging the parent to do most of the talking. If the parent stresses legal involvement, the leader can easily counter by stating, "Well, Mr. Hand, I really would like to continue to discuss this with you to get to some resolution, but I cannot continue if you are going to speak with an attorney . . . the district attorney will have to take it from here."

Most often, this type of response to the parent's idle threat causes him to pause and reevaluate the importance of the school leader's role in correcting any wrongdoing or finding a solution. In many cases, a response to any type of empty promise to elicit some type of response from the leader must be accompanied with the leader staying in complete control.

POLITICAL PARENTS

No educational organization would be complete without the quintessential group of parents who are, or at least think they are, an important piece of the political landscape. Chapter after chapter, it continues to be emphasized that a truly successful leader must learn to become politically savvy but never political. That isn't a fine line to tiptoe around; rather, there is a major difference between making decisions based on favor and quid pro quo and understanding how decisions will affect different bands of stakeholders in your school, district, or organization.

A political response to any school leader dealing with political parents is this: whatever politics seems to be favorable at the moment, a need, decision, or some other type of consideration that may arise from a political parent will most likely change sooner rather than later. School leaders who tie themselves up in any type of political movement almost always fall victim to circumstance as soon as the atmosphere changes. And, yes—it always changes.

Instead, great school leaders can still control and manage local decision making by ensuring that parents with special ties to the policy makers and elected officials in the township are communicated with in a timely manner and accommodated whenever possible in the same manner as other parents. It is important for a leader not to attach her name to the political sides that may present themselves during different times throughout her career.

STAFF RELATIONS

Just as parents may ride the local political wave to curry favor or gain a benefit for their children, a neighbor, close friend, or specific agenda, many faculty, administrators, and staff members also tend to create and attach themselves to specific political factions over their tenure in the district.

Although many of these positions in schools earn tenure and seniority rights either through state legislative statute or via local bargaining agreement, it is inevitable that a staff member who is part of a political arm of the system will be on both the proverbial right and wrong sides of the struggle throughout their time in a district.

A successful school leader identifies these connections and processes how his relationship with the staff member can either support or disrupt both his own agenda and the mission he sets forth for the successful oversight of the organization. A leader must be very careful to consistently ensure that these relationships remain professional but friendly. This can be extremely difficult, especially if the leader has elevated roles within the district.

Being able to navigate through this area effectively can really give the school administrator an advantage when dealing with the local decisions that will ultimately reflect on the operations of the school, district, or organizations. The leader's ability to fully understand her relationship with the individuals closest to her in the trenches can help solidify that an information pipeline will ultimately exist to—and from—her office to those exact individuals she needs to enhance morale and the confidence her teams will have in her leadership.

A good relationship with staff members that is seen by others as a friendship ultimately will lead to an oppositional effect: a barrier will be extended for specific information, and support for certain issues will be kept from the leader and those individuals viewed as her closest allies. This will hurt the leader's ability to show a transparent and fair front when dealing with all individuals under her leadership and their ability to trust her in an open, competitive environment.

LOCAL ELECTED OFFICIALS

The most dangerous stakeholder group to navigate as a school leader to do the most competent job for your students, faculty, families, and staff is local elected officials. This is not to say that all elected officials are difficult to work with. On the contrary, successful elected officials who understand politics and use their political attributes to move a community or city forward are an extremely important part of society.

It's the other individuals who have a political agenda or an overarching expectation with demands and favorable returns the moment they first get elected who should be avoided at all costs. These are elected officials who will never be satisfied with a school leader's performance regardless of the return.

Many school district leaders would argue that besides their board members, local elected officials do not matter much in the overall business of operating the schools. On the surface, this is true. However, looking into the different layers of community involvement, the town/city influencers may easily have a political impact on the school leader and her ability to make a positive impact on her district or organization. Hence, it is important to involve these stakeholders to ensure support for the decisions she needs to make for the smooth, efficient oversight of the educational community.

NAVIGATING YOUR BOARD

An important part of navigating the local politics to ensure that support is obtained for local decisions is working with the board. Elected or appointed, board of education members are inherently attached to specific constituent stakeholder groups that maintain particular agendas throughout the board member's tenure.

Simply put, each board member represents one portion of the educational system to which they were elected or appointed. Thus, in the role as a servant leader, the school administrator must take into account the needs, wants, and asks of board members as they set the vision of the organization. Although a leader must interject her expertise and knowledge base into the decisions as well as recommendations for the efficient operation of the school district, it is ultimately the representative voice of the stakeholders inside that district, township, or organization who will finally determine what is appropriate for the community and what isn't.

Obviously, it is not as simple as this. With the responsibility of governing the schools and representing a percentage of the constituent base in the community, boards of education are charged with ensuring the oversight of the school system and all its moving parts.

Here is where the school leader needs the most support when making decisions that impact the district and community as a whole. Without the majority representation of the individuals he serves, the school leader cannot create a new program, hire the personnel he needs for the district, and definitely not call a snow day!

Chief school administrators know one thing is true: the board who hires you isn't the board who fires you.

When an individual in the field of education is vetted by a team of stakeholders and administrators and ultimately is hired for a position in the district, the administration doesn't hand that individual a welcome packet under the auspices that that teacher will be fired from the school system prior to the start of the next school year. With any new position, the established learning curve is supported by a professional development series, mentoring, and other peer supports to assist new staff with succeeding during their first school year.

Similarly, a school superintendent or chief school administrator understands that the board support received for the hire of a new superintendent is not necessarily the same support given to the superintendent when the names and faces of the board change over the next several years. Understanding and accepting that this may—no, will—occur is an important given that a leader should have when navigating the board and its politics when looking to gain favor and support for decisions that need to be made.

YOU MAKE THE CALL!

You are the high school principal in a suburban school district, and you just received a call from your assistant principal explaining that Anna Q. and Lois J. got into another fistfight in the hallway, the second in three weeks.

Both students are suspended pursuant to the district code of conduct, and your secretary has informed you that an irate Mrs. Q is waiting for you in the main office. As you make your way from the science labs to enter the main hallway, you can hear Mrs. Q screaming at your office personnel in a degrading tone.

Upon entering the office, you immediately receive the brunt of the diatribe, and Mrs. Q states that you cannot keep her daughter safe, and she has already called an attorney to sue the district and you personally. She becomes even more irate when one of your office workers makes a comment under his breath and snickers.

How would you continue to handle the situation? How would you address the parent and your employees?

COACHES' CORNER

1. What decisions would you make in a scenario such as this when a parent threatens you and your authority?
2. Who would you include and/or notify about what occurred?
3. An incident such as this can easily make its way to social media, where only part of the story is told. What can you do to navigate the local politics to ensure that a situation of this nature doesn't hurt your position or reputation?

Chapter 6

Considerations for Polioptics in Local Decision Making

Perception plays an important role in persuading and influencing others to make the best decisions for the educational system or institution. When a school leader is perceived as being knowledgeable or successful in consideration of local issues that involve needed support from stakeholders, the leader has more influence to ensure that her established goals come to fruition. Polioptics is a strategy that school administrators can use to effectuate change in their organization.

POLIOPTICS

Polioptics is the ability to use visual and media-specific aids to relay a message or influence an impact tied to an issue that has political implications in a district, township, city, or organization.

Arguably, every facet of society includes optical measures used to influence market trends or consumers while growing a brand to recognize a mission or goals related to a business, group, or organization. Each optical device allows the team to create a story around a desired need to help grow the organization.

Although very closely related, polioptics should not be confused with most other political actions that take place to either help or harm others for position or power. The ability of a leader to use visual or more personal means to generate support or persuade a cause is an extremely influential tool she should ensure is in her toolkit.

It is also imperative that the school leader understands that she must work with her team in developing a polioptics campaign because it must be delivered in a way that ensures that every angle is covered when attempting to use such means to influence decisions with stakeholders. In other words, polioptic campaigns should not be created or implemented alone. A school leader must use the strengths of each team member to ensure that a solid plan is created to enhance the narrative.

A strong school leader first recognizes that the best polioptic that proves to all stakeholders that she is devoted to any mission or cause is to be visible at as many school, district, or organization events and programs as possible. This seems like a given in considering the expectations of the job itself; however, a school leader must never underestimate the power of influence she will gain by showing interest in the extracurricular side of the school system and what is important to students, staff members, and families outside the school day.

Besides the school leaders' attendance at events, a leader has several other polioptic trends that he can use when to influence stakeholders in the local decisions that impact the educational system he serves.

DATA TRENDS

Whenever possible, a visual representation of data trends should be included in a presentation or as a backdrop to a speech or some type of reporting as evidence to support a projected need or highlight a trend that has impacted stakeholders. Incorporating a longitudinal series of data sets is most beneficial when the school leader wants the average stakeholder to understand how particular patterns of events over time have effective bands of students, staff, and school goals.

Polioptic explanation of trends can be extremely beneficial with discussions that include financial and budgetary concerns, rising/declining enrollment, and of course, assessment scores. It is important for the school leader to include historic data and project pertinent long-term quantitative values to create a definitive, researched-based picture of what any decision may bring to the future educational landscape.

However, most important is that the administrator must not only be able to explain the data he is presenting but also why he is hypothesizing the trends as presented, being able to debate any naysayers who may challenge his theories and the projections as presented.

SOCIAL MEDIA

Social media have brought one of the most influential changes to the educational landscape in modern times. The ability to communicate with stakeholders at a moment's notice in emergency or informational broadcasts has broken communication barriers and provided an informational pipeline for administrators across the country to share ideas and programs for the betterment of schools and districts.

Social media accounts and platforms are also influential polioptic tools for the school leader to gauge support from specific groups of stakeholders for upcoming decisions. However, the school leader must be careful what he posts to these accounts and more importantly, that these account feeds include accurate, up-to-date information. A school administration with a dormant social media account not only seems inefficient but flat out lazy, especially if he has used the platform in the past to assist in pushing his agenda.

Social media applications, forums, and the like are incredible communication tools to establish a quick response/reply avenue that includes the school system and the community it serves. It is a very direct way to get an emergency message out to stakeholders in the quickest way possible, which is very influential when showing all stakeholder groups that the leader has made a final determination on a problem or a process.

With social media, administrators must be mindful of security on the account as well as monitoring responses or replies to messages that may include concerning information or have the potential to spark additional conversations on another issue that may or may not be connected to the discussion at hand. Technological advancements are exponential, and messaging applications include devices that can truly assist the administrator in gathering support and input for decisions that need to be made both on a short- and long-term basis.

BRANDING

In polioptic ranking, branding arguably can be posted at the number one position. Branding aligns directly with perception—how a school system or district is viewed in its mission, color schemes, logo, and mascot are all important to how others view the school system. In turn, the perception of the school district specifically correlates to how others view the township, community, and those individual students, faculty, and staff members who walk the hallways of the school buildings.

A district or school system's mission statement should be reviewed every five years to ensure that the mission and vision align closely with the sitting board members who each represent one fraction of the school community it serves. The mission statement must also reflect the expectations of the educational system for its students, be a compelling statement, and offer a unique perspective on the future of the community.

Every school system or district has a mascot that represents the qualities and values of the community as a whole. Some educational systems may have one overall representation of school pride for the community, with each individual site having its own mascot to represent a local or neighborhood mission for each school. Regardless of the makeup, school mascots provide the greatest polioptic influence on how stakeholders come together to support the decisions made for their local schools or schools that they attended.

With this type of branding comes the absolute need to ensure that perception rises to the greatest expectation and surpasses a standard of excellence second to none. Logo design, apparel, postings and signage on facilities, sharp images, and so forth lend incredible value to the success of the administration in charge. When the appearance or the outside perception of an organization exceeds every expectation level, the perception is that the organization exceeds its potential in all areas.

Take, for example, district signage. A visitor from a city one hour away comes to a high-school campus to watch his niece play a basketball game on a Thursday afternoon. Upon his arrival, parking spaces are limited because it is a weekday, and meetings are held after students' dismissal. The parking lots have very limited signage, and he is unsure which door to use to enter the gymnasium.

As he finds parking in the south lot, he notices a visitor's parking sign, but it is bent and twisted and cannot be viewed from the roadway. On the side of the retaining wall in front of his parking spot is graffiti that includes profanity.

The first impression for this visiting uncle and the perception of the district is most likely negative. Further, the lack of concern for the aesthetics of the campus automatically transfers to the perceived notion of a lack of concern for what is happening inside as well. This would include the academic program of the district, the individuals who attend and work at the schools, and most definitely the school administrators charged with leading the school district.

In turn, the visiting uncle's impression of how the schools are run now moves to the township. Graffiti, students acting poorly in a social setting, and other adverse events create a view of the district that does not help the school leader gain support when making local decisions, enhancing programs, or working for the betterment of the school system.

Appropriate branding is an integral part of school district identity for present, past, and future generations of students in any educational system. Done the correct way, branding can be used as a polioptic tool for a school administrator who wishes to enhance the level of pride in his school system so stakeholders rally around his decisions, goals, and action plans. This makes the local decision-making process easier and more palpable to those who are most affected by those decisions. Polioptic tools can strengthen the trust between a leader and the community he serves if used consistently and correctly.

YOU MAKE THE CALL!

Dr. Jennifer Stronge has been the educational leader of the Northfield Independent Schools District for the past eight years and recently secured funding to restructure one of the high-school gymnasiums destroyed by a flood.

During the design process, Dr. Stronge received feedback from the school principal and student government representatives that they would like to add a more modern looking mascot to the gym floor, and the superintendent discussed the layout with the board's facilities committee.

After the new gym floor was revealed at the first home basketball game, many school alumni were enraged that the logo looked different than it was when the school first adopted it in 1973. The superintendent received correspondence from former graduates and local community members about how unhappy they were with the change.

Although Dr. Stronge had support from the current stakeholders at the school and the board, what are her next steps in attempting to regain support from other members of the school and district? What could she have done differently to ensure that politics wouldn't be involved in the local decision-making process?

COACHES' CORNER

Activity

Choose a school or district and outline a rebranding campaign. What steps would you take to change the perception of the organization in a positive manner? Who would you involve in the process? What factors do you need to consider when enhancing the polioptics (equity, finances, traditions, etc.)?

Chapter 7

Forming Local Alliances

It can be argued that forming alliances with local agencies, organizations, and groups is the most important task that an educational leader has during her tenure in a district, building, or institution of higher education. A successful administrator incorporates intricate strategies to form alliances with stakeholders and individuals who hold positions of power in a community or organization. It is imperative for a leader to familiarize herself with as many strategies as possible to strengthen local community alliances because not every strategy will work with every community member or stakeholder group.

Making a strong partnership with members of the local community is one definitive way that a school chief, district leader, or building supervisor can gain information and support when it comes to making decisions that affect the township, school district, or the organization. To form successful alliances with local entities, a school leader should take several key steps.

KNOW THE IMPORTANCE OF THE ALLIANCE

After recognizing the need for an alliance with a specific individual or group, the school leader must quickly ascertain its importance. This recognition is twofold. First, what is the importance of the alliance to the school system; and second, how is the alliance important to the leader in his role?

A school leader must ensure that she aligns herself with individuals or groups who represent and support the mission of the schools and, at the same time, will not compromise the political capital she has already worked so hard to gain. By vetting the individual or group she wants to align with, the administrator fully understands who or what she is getting involved with.

Will such an alliance impact her education in a positive manner and help her gain the support she needs when making decisions, building programs, or adding important initiatives? On the other hand, would such an alliance with this individual or group push away other important supporters or attenuate their level of support in a way that is detrimental to the progress she has already made?

The leader must also consider how the alliance will benefit her as an individual both personally and professionally. This consideration must not only be made in terms of her current position but her future career goals as well. Aligning oneself with an individual or a group that is political in nature or extremely controversial can lead to a compromising position.

KNOW THE HISTORY OF THE INDIVIDUAL OR GROUP WITH WHOM YOU ARE ALIGNING

As part of the vetting process for any alliance that a school leader would consider, an in-depth review of the history of the individual or group and their impact on and connection to the local school system is extremely important. By using current members of her team, her board, and allies currently in place, the school leader must carefully navigate the historical investigation to include present ties to the education system and past controversies with previous school leaders, board trustees, administrators, or school employees.

The school leader should fully understand how a potential partnership with such an individual or group could impact her role as a leader in the community and the mission of the school system both positively and negatively. Does the positive implication that an alliance brings with it outweigh the potential downfall or negative outlook? Will current board supporters and members of the leadership team view the alliance as a poor decision based on past experiences and outcomes?

It is important that negative impacts from historical experiences never creep back into a school system. As it normally takes several cycles of elections and a generation of students to move away from a distinct memory of poor decisions, bad leadership, or political bosses from the past, a strong review of the historic relationship with others is a must in ensuring that the right alliances are courted and can assist in strengthening the support that the school leader will have throughout her organization.

The historical context is even more important so that the school leader is fully aware of the potential fallout or impact that any such alliance will have on her tenure in the position. Even though such a partnership may have been unstable or volatile in the distant past, it may be necessary for the school administrator to align once again with an individual or organization if it will potentially benefit the current goals and mission of the district or school system.

WHO ARE THE IMPORTANT PLAYERS?

For many school chiefs and administrators, it is easy to identify the individuals and organizations that are important to partner with in gaining support for making decisions and moving the mission of the schools forward. The greater task is to pinpoint the most important players within those ranks.

Successfully securing an alliance within a school system absolutely takes the leader using a top-down approach. He must first make contact and enter informal discussions with the head of the group or the most vocal and outspoken stakeholder to then have everyone onboard with the partnership.

If the leader chose instead to maneuver from the bottom up, he would have informed conversations that would splinter into different viewpoints and fracture the message to the benefit of the individual, group, or organization he was looking to align with. Rather, by fostering ties first with the key player (or players), he allows those individuals to approach their constituents in a manner they see fit to get the message across. The group may discuss or argue among themselves; however, majority support ultimately will return to the key members with a compromise that most likely is acceptable to everyone involved.

IDENTIFY POTENTIAL QUID PRO QUO

A politically savvy school leader always knows that with every ask comes a potential favor in return. This is a typical negotiating tactic as long as it meets every moral, ethical, and legal standard prescribed for the situation at hand.

If the school leader has been elevated to his position through the ranks, then he definitely understands that alliances are symbiotic and are most successful when the tenets of the partnership are fully presented before the alliance begins. As this is common in every relationship, awareness of what is being asked in return is the most pressing part of ensuring that the school leader maintains the upper hand in controlling the alliance.

WHAT ARE THE PARAMETERS OF THE PARTNERSHIP?

As each alliance brings with it the possibility of important advantages to the school leader in consideration of influencing the decision-making process, the school leader must dissect each possible relationship to fully understand what parameters define the desired outcomes. The school leader must quickly acknowledge what the potential alliance will bring to his career trajectory in his current position and beyond.

The leader must fully understand the parameters of the relationship prior to committing to the alliance. This includes any expectation of what the partnership will need in return and any time lines connected to such requests. Often, a true alliance will establish a positive working relationship that lends support for an extended period.

The leader must also be very aware of how the different allies he makes interact with each other. This is necessary to ensure that he can remove himself from possible future disputes or miscommunication between the allies. It's imperative that the leader stay neutral in any disagreements, or he may lose several alliances even if he is not directly involved in the disagreement.

EXPLAIN WHAT YOU NEED—BE SPECIFIC

Creating strong alliances includes getting directly to the point. The individuals or organizations the school leader chooses to include in such partnerships must know the specific needs and the varying degrees of support that the leader expects to have in consideration of the bond that is formed. This is not to suggest that anything considered would not meet any moral, ethical, or legal standard or would be part of an unimaginable quid pro quo.

Rather, every alliance in a school system depends on a symbiotic relationship among all members. This is how such an alliance continues to grow strong and make positive change in a school system or educational organization. As all the moving parts work together to meet the goal of each member of the partnership, it is crucial that the specific needs of each partner are made known and it is specified how the other partners can assist him/her in meeting those goals.

Being specific most importantly includes future expectations of the partnership. A truly strong, dedicated alliance can withstand disagreements, differences of opinion, and the potential for political hurdles from time to time. In fact, these types of challenges, at times, can help strengthen the partnership as the parameters and needs of the members continue to grow for the sake of the individuals involved and the organizations they represent.

In school systems, important alliances sometimes have a "time stamp": elections can change the makeup of boards, new positions and promotions bring different professionals to the system, and stakeholder members (such as PTA liaisons) change as students graduate from districts or families move from township or city boundaries. Thus, a school leader's ability to understand the needs of her partners and the timeliness of those outcomes is most beneficial when creating such partnerships in the first place.

YOU MAKE THE CALL!

As the school principal of Horten Elementary Magnet School, Ms. Pappandrikos has fostered a strong relationship with the Home and School Association president. Both she and the president meet on a weekly basis, and the two have been spotted having lunch at a bistro in a neighboring town on a Saturday afternoon.

Recently, Ms. Pappandrikos received a fund-raiser request from the band parents' association to host a festival in the school auditorium on a Sunday morning. Ms. Pappandrikos denied the request because custodians do not work on Sundays, and a custodian must be present in the building for health and safety purposes and boiler duty.

Word got back to the principal from the district chief administrator that she denied the request because the band parent chairman and the Home and School Association president do not get along with one another, and recently they had an argument in the school parking lot. The rumor is spreading very quickly around the community.

What should the principal do to help rectify the situation? What can Ms. Pappandrikos do going forward to ensure that she keeps her alliances free from scrutiny and possible animosity?

COACHES' CORNER

1. Think about a local alliance that you have with an individual or group in your school, district, or organization. What are some parameters and boundaries of the alliance?
2. For the alliance in the previous question, do others know of your relationship? If so, how has it affected your professional relationship with others regarding the alliance itself? If others don't know, why not?
3. What factors may cause an educational leader to remove herself from a local alliance?

Chapter 8

Building Partnerships

We just reviewed the importance of forming alliances with different stakeholders of the education system to ensure that a school leader has the support and understanding of key stakeholders within the community when considering local decisions that will impact the school system both as a whole and in specific situations. As forming local alliances will prove to be beneficial to the overall success of the school leader, her ability to formulate partnerships that will create such an alliance is the most important way to gain support and respect for the decisions that she will make.

The school leader must continuously work to build strong partnerships with her constituent base and the appropriate stakeholders. In doing so, she has protocols and administrative tools she can use to make this a very attainable goal.

BE YOURSELF

It seems simple enough, but a leader must always remember to be himself when interacting with others, especially when building relationships. Trying to invent a persona or have others perceive that the leader may know more about a topic than he does will prevent the partnership from flourishing into what is truly needed when gathering strong allies to stand behind him in times of need.

Individuals need to see their leaders as genuine. As easy as it is to identify a leader's strengths and positive qualities, it is even more important for others to recognize where a leader may be vulnerable. This is where partners can understand that the growing relationship is wholly symbiotic, and each individual needs the other in some manner to strengthen ties.

GAIN TRUST

A school leader's ability to be open and transparent with others is the only way to gain trust in a school district or educational organization. Most leaders only have ties to the educational community based on the professional part of their résumé. In other words, unless the administrator lives in the township or city he serves or is an alum of that institution, school, or district, his vested interest relies solely on professional capital he has built, or intends to build, while serving in an administrative capacity.

Although it truly isn't, this can be seen as a negative if the school leader doesn't work to gain the full trust of the constituents to whom he is accountable every day. Challenges in the trust area include tax impact as it relates to budget spending, the community engagement the leader commits to throughout his tenure, and the connections he makes with parents, students, and other groups attached to the school community.

The school administrator will only be seen as trustworthy if she remains consistent and leads by example in order to ensure a strong alliance. Take, for example, a school principal handling evaluations with her faculty and staff.

In the beginning of the year, the principal sets high expectations for her staff to consider when delivering instruction to students in an elementary school. She offers her faculty a set of goals and explains that everyone will work together to meet them. She further states that she will hold everyone accountable for doing their part in producing the best results for the students.

The school year moves forward, and faculty and staff members work together and develop professionally to meet the goals that the principal set forth. At the start, morale is high, and several veteran teachers are excited that the school will be back on track to create a conducive, challenging learning environment for all students.

The work isn't easy. Teachers are spending their free time reviewing supplemental training tools and working hard to incorporate the newest learning modalities to put the theories they are learning into practice while differentiating instruction for each learner in their classroom.

Most of the teachers and support staff continue to go above and beyond to reach and even surpass the goals that the leader set in September. However, a small facet of teachers disagree with the changes being implemented and they are not in favor of the extra time that they need to put in to establish new techniques and protocols. They are also arguing with many of the teachers working to meet the new goals because they feel that those are just another attempt to blame the teaching staff, rather than lack of support from the administration, for poor test scores.

The principal does the best she can to ensure that all the teachers and staff members are working together to meet the goals. For the first four months of the school year, she pinpoints the team members who are working to reach the desired goal and those who are continuously setting hurdles to hinder others while doing minimal work themselves. It had become obvious over time which students are performing better with the new rigorous demands on the curriculum and accompanying assessments and which students are still behind the benchmarks set in September.

As the first half of the year is coming to a close, the principal completes her evaluation rounds for the teachers in her building. As is the case with every evaluation rubric and model, every teacher is assessed on the same tenets of instruction and program, student engagement, and subject/grade specific aptitude. The principal completes the evaluations in two weeks and discusses her findings with teachers and staff members in post conferences.

This scenario is real and familiar to every sitting school administrator regardless of the type of district or education system they serve. It is the next action of the principal that will decide whether she gains the trust of her team and is seen as a true leader for her building and those teachers and staff members for whom she is responsible.

After several weeks of evaluations and post conferences, conversations start in the faculty lounge. It quickly becomes apparent that most, if not all, faculty and staff members who were resisting the changes and not performing tasks to meet the administrator's established goals have received the same ratings as the teachers who were feverishly working to advance instruction and meet tight deadlines to meet the principal's charge.

In fact, the principal is overheard discussing some veteran teacher evaluations with the assistant principal, and she states that she wouldn't feel right giving a veteran teacher of fifteen years who has always had outstanding evaluations a "needs improvement" right now. Whether or not this is confirmed, the perception becomes real. Supporters of the principal and her goals are not only hurt by such actions, but they are devastated by the disrespect she has shown in not holding others accountable for their actions.

In effect, the school principal has lost the respect, support, and the trust of her teachers—her partners in the trenches—due to her inability to lead effectively and hold accountable those who are not doing their best to meet the goals. Through this one act, the principal lost the ability to engage or motivate any teacher to surpass a productivity goal in the near or distant future because simply put, the principal doesn't seem to value the time and effort the majority of the teachers put forth due to her inability to hold others accountable.

What should have occurred? The principal should have been a true leader and held everyone accountable for the task with which they were charged.

Just as her faculty and staff members trusted her with the direction she was taking them in when she set forth the new goals and objectives in early September, the principal put her trust in her faculty and staff to ensure that they would work through any difficulties to meet the new standards. The expectation from faculty or staff is that any effective leader would give a seasoned or veteran teacher a rating that he deserves. A merit-based evaluation would have set an amazing tone in that building, indicating that all individuals were being held accountable for their actions.

Because trust is a two-way street, the actions of a school leader in any given situation will cause his faculty and staff to either trust him or not when he makes the next decision. When a leader is consistent, holds others accountable, and truly models the expectations he has for others, he leads his subordinates to trust in his decision-making process. Regardless of whether his constituents agree with his decision or accept its outcome, they will still appreciate and respect that he has established a consistent set of expectations and boundaries for all members of his team—not just some members—which will lead to stronger partnerships and greater support in the long run.

LISTEN MORE . . . SPEAK MUCH LESS

It is much easier for a school leader or administrator to build a partnership base when he listens to the needs of his partners rather than constantly asking for something in return. In fact, a good school leader can get his needs across to his constituent base without them knowing how much he needs their support. The administrator can do this through programmatic changes, impromptu meetings with stakeholders, or hosting community events to spotlight the achievements of students and the community as a whole.

Great leaders are great listeners. By listening to a stakeholder, a school leader not only lets that individual know that the individual's issue is extremely important, but also that the leader has a vested interest in seeing that the problem, concern, or idea presented is considered and reacted to in a timely fashion. Engaging others by listening instead of always dominating the dialogue allows the potential partner to feel empowered to become part of the decision-making process.

Listening is a very important skill in strengthening the role of partners within any alliance. Although the school administrator may be the best leader or most educated individual in the room, when it comes to the level playing field in a partnership, listening to all parties allows the administrator to control the narrative and the situation at hand much more than the other included parties. Basically, knowing when to speak is more important than speaking often.

Here's a good example of what not to do: the school leader hosts a weekly meeting with his leadership team, faculty, and so forth for no other reason than holding a weekly meeting. A leader must never appear to be speaking only to hear himself speak. Delivering a mundane message to a group of individuals that could easily have been relayed individually only proves to the leader's base that their time is not valuable or that the leader needs to ensure that everyone knows that he's in charge.

Conversely, calling a group meeting sparingly, only when action needs to be taken or conversations need to be had, gives the meeting more value. The impact is more significant both on the individuals and the partnership, which is being strengthened from losing the notion that "we are just meeting to meet." Allowing partners to experience firsthand how the school leader is mindful of their time, productivity, and their concerns without always expecting something in return is an important way to build the partnership.

DO YOUR PART

Psychologists and counselors have been known to say that a relationship only works if each party truly puts in 100 percent of the effort 100 percent of the time. This quantified definition is true for the relationship that school administrators have with the stakeholder groups they represent and their colleagues.

Some of the most successful leaders in the global marketplace and across all industries do an incredible job of making others feel like they are the most important individuals in the room. This leadership characteristic is an imperative building block in ensuring that the leader values his relationship with others at the early stages of the relationship building itself.

Great partners care deeply about the needs of their counterparts. Sometimes, the effort of care carries over so much that the leader's needs and perspective take a backseat to strengthen the partnership.

STRONG COMMUNICATION

It is difficult to imagine that any partnership would survive without strong communication among all the partners. In reality, communication must come from all sides for the partnership to be truly successful and transparent.

Some communication vehicles are simple, whereas others sometimes seem to be more difficult for school leaders to grasp. For example, a school administrator can easily build a partnership with parents when communicating to them about the upcoming band concert, then nearly sever ties with staff as she fails to inform them that a new textbook series was chosen for next year.

When it comes to challenges, programs, and protocols that will at some point reach the public and be scrutinized by one or more stakeholder groups, a school leader knows that getting the information out to stakeholders prior before it gets out on its own may cause less confusion and avoid potential problems that may come from outside influencers based on the lack of or untimely dissemination of the communication itself.

The school leader must always be careful what information he gives to stakeholders when he communicates about an action or occurrence. Thus, all communications must be cleared by an administrator or school leader at the top of the organization or the district legal counsel prior to sending it out to the masses. Conversely, sending out the wrong message can be detrimental to the communication threads already in place and working effectively.

SET GOALS

Partnerships grow strong when the individuals involved know that they are striving to reach a common goal (or goals) and they are aware of the action plans put in place as a roadmap to ensure that the goal is attainable. Goals establish a purpose for the partnership in consideration of each partner involved and how the goal will affect change for the individual and group if/when the goal is reached.

Setting goals also allows for practice in strengthening communication among members of the partnership where dialogue includes the needs and concerns of each partner. By setting and then communicating through a goal, there is enough common ground to strengthen the partnership in consideration of what each individual needs. As school leaders understand, the more individuals working together with a shared vision, the greater the support when decisions need to be made.

A school administrator can use a goal-setting standard to help mitigate negative feedback from a decision he makes that will affect other stakeholder groups. As he gains support from some of his closest constituents, the school leader is prepared to engage in conversation around what his goal was when considering all the possible outcomes of that decision.

RESPECT

In any career position, field, or industry, leaders can only gain the respect of stakeholders through mutual respect. This is a main consideration when a school leader wants support for her suggestions, initiatives, and the programs she puts forth for her district, school, or organization. At times, this might be a difficult undertaking for a school administrator because a school system is an easy target for disrespectful tendencies from stakeholder groups and the public.

At times, dealing with parents concerning issues with their child lends itself to difficult conversations as parents come to a student's defense. Further, where monies are intermingled with salaries, benefits, and so forth, public stakeholder groups tend to believe that they have a stronghold on the decisions that educational administration, faculty, and staff make daily.

Interactions, at times, come across as disrespectful and disrupt the progress school leaders have made with specific sections of the district and school community. When parents and other engaged groups feel slighted or disrespected due to dealings with their children or themselves, communication becomes choppy, perception is that the administrator is picking on specific students, and respect—on both sides—diminishes.

When a school leader sees that an incident or concern is heading toward hindering the respect one group has for the other, she must immediately immerse herself in the situation and ensure that the problem is rectified before it has a negative outcome. By respecting others, the partnership remains strong and invulnerable to outside influences or threats.

BE FLEXIBLE AND FAIR

No individual wants to create or maintain a partnership with someone who presents herself as inflexible or unfair. A partnership, by definition, is a give-and-take relationship where each individual works to maintain specific parameters so that other individuals in the partnership succeed.

Each member also needs to be fair and consistent when dealing with each member of the partnership and what she represents in relation to the district or organization. In other words, one partner's cause is no greater or no less concerning than that of any other partner. Fairness includes the idea that each member receives the same level of benefit from the relationship as long as he gives back the same level of benefit.

STAY HUMBLE

Great school leaders humble themselves and let their stakeholders take most of the credit for the work and the progress that is accomplished. Although it may be an individual's "calling" to be a school administrator, it is still his job. Performing his job correctly is tied to a compensation package that allows the leader to provide for himself and his family.

If the school leader builds strong relationships in a proper way, the successes will spotlight his involvement with the work and progress that continues to occur long after he leaves the district or organization. By staying humble, the leader proves to others that this success is just one stop in a long path to achieving greatness and it can only be done with the partnerships that have been created and that are now highlighted.

YOU MAKE THE CALL!

Dr. Freed meets his faculty at the first meeting of the year in September. He has decided that he will lay down the law at the beginning of the year and have teachers establish three SMART goals to hold them accountable for increasing test scores. Dr. Freed starts the meeting by explaining that he has been admonished by the superintendent for the lack of productivity in the building, and he is "no longer going to get in trouble for the lack of work being produced" by only a few teachers on staff in the building.

What has Dr. Freed created at the beginning of the school year? How could he have gotten his message across a little better? What has this introduction done for any alliance that may already have been established or potential alliances?

COACHES' CORNER

1. Discuss a time when a school leader admonished an entire team or faculty but it truly was directed only at several individuals. What did such a conversation do for productivity? For morale?
2. Why are partnerships so crucial when wanting to remove politics from local decisions that need to be made?
3. Describe a time when a partnership or relationship of yours went wrong. Were you able to repair it? If so, what tools did you use?

Chapter 9

Directed Informational Leadership

Directed informational leadership is a leadership style that educational administrators use to guide decisions and demands of stakeholder groups. This type of leadership is pertinent to a leader's success in gaining support for decisions he makes for the local education system that will impact the entire community.

Transformational leaders move their organization forward. These leaders inspire those in their charge to effect change by motivating others and becoming part of the entire educational process. Directed informational leadership styles provide pathways for stakeholders to ensure support for local decisions that a school leader must make to advance the organization as she sees fit. These pathways act as a guide for stakeholders that allow them to feel confident that they are an important part of the process while providing the administrator with a livable outcome based on the needs of the organization.

Providing a roadmap for stakeholders to assist the leader in making decisions is a crucial component in leading an education system. Further, when it comes to making both everyday and long-term decisions that ultimately affect the students, their families, and the community as a whole, gaining the perspective of the important stakeholder groups is important in ensuring not only that the parameters of the decision are best for all involved but that they are sustainable.

Why is sustainability in directed informational strategies so important? Easily stated, building any program should be structured so that it will thrive and prosper not only year after year but long after you leave the position or transfer to a new district or organization. Too often, leaders neglect to address or put in place sustainable efforts to maintain programs that are created, so all the work and efforts from administration, teachers, and other stakeholder groups are lost. This not only hurts programmatic stability within an organization, but it also shines a negative light on how the school leadership team feels about the effort put forth by stakeholder group members and the success of programs in the district.

A leader who uses a directed informational style to guide the important decisions of the district or organization also understands that she must research several outcomes and be prepared to answer all stakeholder concerns about each scenario prior to her bringing those suggestions to the fore. This style cannot be effective if the leader only researches and provides one possible solution for the group to consider as it deliberates the pros and cons for a particular program that will come from the work of the group.

The following steps can help a school administrator extend some of his influence on stakeholder groups assisting the leader in making an informed decision based on directed informational leadership.

RESEARCH SEVERAL OUTCOMES

The ultimate key when using directed informational leadership to influence a group is for the administrator to identify and fully research several outcomes that she can agree with. In other words, regardless of the decision of the group or stakeholder committee that has deliberated to choose the best program, book, curriculum, and so on, the school leader will be amenable to the recommended outcome.

Although transparency is extremely important when working alongside stakeholder groups, it is a best practice consideration that during this type of process, stakeholders don't recognize that all the possibilities the leader sets forth are decisions that she has chosen. The leader must show that she would support any of the suggestions she has set forth because she has vetted each of the outcomes. The leader should also consider describing one or several other possibilities that were researched and proven not to be conducive to a positive experience for the students and families in the community.

Here, she must use caution and not come off like this is her own agenda. Rather, since the leader will be seeing the decision take shape and come to fruition under her charge, she must show the group that she is willing to accept whatever decision comes forth as long as she has their complete support.

The research the leader collected must be provided to the team and tangible enough so that the positive and negative outcomes can be presented in a compare-and-contrast format so the group may weigh all outcomes. Key for the school administrator is to get the group to agree that any of the suggested outcomes will greatly serve the community. When this occurs, the whole group feels passionate about the decision to be made because there are no bad decisions, only one decision that is better than the next.

PRIORITIZE THE SPECIFIED OUTCOMES

Although a strong educational leader will take her recommendations and gain stakeholder buy-in with each scenario, she ultimately will prefer one product, program, or policy change over another. Priority stacking occurs when a leader takes all the supported outcomes and arranges them in theory from highest to lowest priority.

To stack any group of outcomes in an appropriate manner, the school leader must ask herself the who, how, and the why of all the possible outcomes selected. From there, she can formulate a strong priority order that she can work on to justify the group's decisions while supporting her needs as well.

For the "who," the leader must identify who the decision making will support; more important, will it affect the leader herself? This can focus on time, political considerations, compensation, or confidence growth from other stakeholder groups. Priority usually leans in favor of those instances where more individuals can be affected positively by a particular decision. Decisions that have little impact on multiple groups within the community most likely have a smaller stake in the order.

The "how" introduces procedures and protocols that the leader may use to ensure that she can accomplish the task at hand. Higher priority decisions most likely include fewer avenues to tackle in consideration of how the team will get to the desired outcome. The how is further dissected through reviewing time on task, number of individuals needed to complete the task, the workload of those individuals, and other areas of the district or organization that will be affected by the decision.

As for the "why," it is imperative that the leader fully understands what is at stake and what the possible outcomes will be should she prevail—a successful project or initiative or not. Basically, "why are we doing this?" The leader should always reach one step further and ask herself: What will be the impact of this decision on my students five, ten, and fifteen years from now?

Using these guiding questions, the school leader can prioritize which decision would be better suited for her to implement in the district or organization, even though any of the choices proposed would be acceptable. Knowing what the priority order entails for her leadership role and the workload that comes with it gives the leader the ability to steer stakeholders in the appropriate direction when formulating decisions and answering concerns.

IDENTIFY STAKEHOLDERS WHO WILL LEAD

As soon as possible, the leader must identify individuals in her stakeholder groups who can lead others effectively. This usually comes from the leader observing group members in other roles and interactions outside the walls of the school buildings and district offices. The ability to align with those who can put themselves in a position to not only back the leader but the program or idea as well is an extremely important part of the process.

After identifying those members of the group or committee who can take charge, the administrator must ensure that that individual takes an active communication role throughout the process. This means that the individual should be encouraged to contribute during meetings and work alongside the administrator outside any official meeting capacity. This will allow the stakeholder/leader to influence the group and gain support for the priority program that the school leader would like the group to recommend.

IDENTIFY STAKEHOLDERS WHO WILL CHALLENGE

It is just as important for a school leader to identify those members of a stakeholder group or community committee who tend to challenge nearly every aspect of the group's mission. No single committee could be productive without including individuals who are on opposing sides of the decision-making process. The interactions within committees that include this type of arrangement tend to produce the most thorough and engaging programs, based solely on the feedback obtained through discussions and the exchanges from one group to the next.

Knowing immediately which members of the group will challenge any direction the leader chooses is important when providing the most influential and directed pathways to progress. The directed informational style invites these individuals to offer their concerns publicly so that the leader can address them. Further, if the individual challenging the point decides to challenge all the information gathered with regard to all possible scenarios, it weakens the challenger's hold on the situation since he just disagrees with everything suggested. Although this may not be witnessed too frequently in the educational arena, it serves its purpose when trying to show that an individual may not have the best interests of the students, staff, and district families in mind.

PERSUADE THROUGH INFLUENCE

Once the recommendations have been researched and set forth and the group dynamics identified, the leader who is playing the directed informational role must use her influential leadership style to persuade the group that one of the recommendations must be supported to move the district or organization forward.

Along with her ability to use the human capital she has already obtained in her current role, she can use the research on each recommendation to push through her list in priority order. She can further influence the decision coming from the committee by ensuring that all members have their say on each recommendations and that they are provided answers to follow-up questions or concerns they may have.

ASSIST IN THE FOLLOW-THROUGH

Now that the recommendations have been vetted, the committee or group has met, and the leader has successfully navigated the group to support what has been brought forward, the leader must follow through to close the sale. This final step is important in the directed informational process: it allows the stakeholder group or committee members to feel that their efforts have not gone unnoticed and the leader to feel that her needs have been met.

In this step, it is very important that the administrator follows through so that the initiative doesn't stall when it lands on another administrator's desk or other questions need to be answered before the recommendation is given full approval. Once again, as this is the most important part of the process, it is also arguably the most overlooked part of the process. Without the appropriate follow-through and support, the leader will be unable to secure the support that she had previously gained from the stakeholders in the community.

Directed informational leadership is not a way to trick or deceive constituents. Rather, an educational leader must use this style to ensure that the appropriate programs, policies, products, and curricular considerations are being used in the educational system. As stakeholder groups consist of members from a wide cross-section of a community, their taking part and having a say in all decisions that impact the educational system is imperative to receiving support for the local decisions made to run the school district effectively.

The expectation of most members of a community is that the school leaders have a strong aptitude in dealing with the academic, social and emotional, extracurricular, athletic, and career readiness needs of the students they serve. Thus, preparing and suggesting several pathways available to a district or community with the support of individuals who support those community groups should be the expected way that school leaders lead a school district.

The directed informational style of leadership allows the school leader to take what he understands about the needs of his students and their families and establish action plans for goals set by the community leaders who are either elected or appointed by the stakeholders themselves. This complete checks-and-balances approach lends itself to ensuring that everyone has a seat at the table and the decisions are based solely on what is best for the students.

YOU MAKE THE CALL!

As the supervisor of elementary mathematics in the Beck County Public Schools, Eddie Laz has been told by the chief administrator that the board expects a recommendation for a new textbook series and accompanying online modules by the February budget hearing. Mr. Laz had already done research on a new series and has discussed the pros and cons for several of the choices with colleagues in neighboring cities and around the country.

After a thorough review, he feels that the math general and mathematics pro programs would be the best fit for the students in the district. After meeting with the chief administrator, she agrees with Ed, and he begins to follow the district protocols and procedures for adopting a new textbook. He forms his committee, and the process begins.

What steps should he take to ensure that he receives input from his committee but also directs the conversation?

COACHES' CORNER

1. Describe a time when you used a directed informational leadership style to assist in making a local decision.
2. How does an educational leader ensure that her stakeholders feel that their input is valued and will be used?
3. What other strategies can a leader use to influence decisions that may include political influence?

Chapter 10

Stakeholders as Defined in Educational Settings

Every field includes important stakeholders that a leader must work alongside to ensure success and productivity throughout the organization. For many leaders, the most important stakeholders are grouped as employees, customers, or investors.

Stakeholders support the daily operations of a system by ensuring that the established mission continues to move forward in which each individual plays his part in meeting that mission. Without support from these groups, the mission ultimately will be unsuccessful as workplace morale will suffer along with any possibility of increasing the organization's productivity.

It is imperative for an educational leader to identify and understand the underlying needs of all stakeholders within an educational organization, school building, or an institution of higher education. From students to custodians to government officials, every decision the administrator makes has a different outcome for each stakeholder group.

STUDENTS

Arguably the most important stakeholders in the education arena, the students must be considered the top priority when the educational leader is making decisions that impact the educational system. Regardless of the student's age, grade band, classification, or standing in the district, a true leader recognizes that equity in access is the most important way to get students what they need in the most efficient way possible.

How to Manage These Stakeholders Effectively

Although they are students, they are the most important group in the organization. Therefore, they should have a say in all matters pertaining to the education system. Of course, in a PK–12 setting, the majority are still minors, and certain decisions cannot include their input or desired outcome. For the most part, however, choices and decisions that will affect the students' everyday school experience and morale should include groups or panels for the administrator to receive feedback prior to making a decision.

This could include meeting with the student government organization to discuss district events, a youth advisory committee (YAC) to assist with menu choices in the cafeterias, random student volunteers to discuss dress code issues, and building liaisons to assist with community events and other concerns that come up from time to time.

PARENTS

Twenty-first century, post-COVID-19 parents are heavily invested in the daily opportunities that their child has in a school system. Parents present the loudest voice when it comes to the educational system in their city or township. First, the school system and what it offers is a major reason why they chose to live in the community or remain part of it for many years. They understand the value that the school system brings to their child, their family, and the community as a whole.

As they are completely invested in what the system can offer their son or daughter, they must be wholly comfortable with the individuals responsible for their health and safety. Everything beyond that is secondary in the eyes of this stakeholder group.

With that charge also comes the importance of how the educational leader holds herself. Is she indecisive, or can she make informed decisions in a timely manner? Is she consistent with her discipline and following the policies as outlined by the school district? Does she have empathy, and can she show understanding and be supportive at times when the community needs that commitment?

Without these things, the educational leader will not gain the support of the parents in the district or the school she serves. The students and their parents/guardians make up the nucleus of the system. It is imperative that the leader works to ensure that an open line of communication exists and is operational with these stakeholders.

How to Manage These Stakeholders Effectively

Communication with parents is essential to ensuring that you have the support of this stakeholder group when decisions need to be made on specific topics throughout the school year. Parents may not always agree with the decision that you make, but if it is in the best interest of their child, then it is difficult for any group to sustain an argument.

However, if the decision is not communicated in almost an immediate manner, or if input from parents is not gathered before the decision is made, the leader has lost a major part of the support he had because he kept the group distant from the entire process. So many methods of disseminating information and receiving feedback are available that the educational leader who desires to remain transparent or inform stakeholder groups when the need arises truly has no excuse not to do so.

To reach this stakeholder group, the school leader should use social media platforms, hold open forum evenings to discuss important or controversial topics, consider posting a video message, present the community with a newsletter or blog, and conduct surveys to gather quantitative data on specific informational trends that become important to the decision-making process.

Most importantly, the educational leader must connect with parent organizations and understand what their needs are in anticipation of any future decisions that need to be considered when making changes to the district, school, or organization. These parent groups should not be limited to only the PTO (parent/teacher organization), HSA (home and school association), or PTA (parent/teacher association), but include groups where parents are involved in areas of major influence around the community such as booster clubs, band associations, green team, local recreation sports, project graduation, and MADD (Mothers Against Drunk Driving). Connecting with present, past, and future parents through group affiliations allows for an appropriate flow of information and lets parents get to know the administrator on a different level.

FACULTY AND STAFF

Yes, those individuals in the trenches are an extremely important stakeholder group that must be considered and included when the important decisions are being made by the educational leaders of the district.

A smart educational leader understands that he can only be seen as successful if his teachers are successful. It is imperative that the administrator listen for cues relative to morale or uneasiness. If an issue arises, the leader must be able to identify and address it immediately.

How to Manage These Stakeholders Effectively

Communication is key! Keeping an open line of communication between the teachers and the administrator is the only way to continuously take the pulse of the district and truly understand the needs and wants of the teachers themselves.

ADMINISTRATION

To the educational leader, her core administrative team is important to the oversight and direction of the district. Her team must also be in step with each decision she makes during the school year. The educational leader must surround herself with a team of leaders with diverse skills to complement the areas of expertise where she may be lacking. By creating a team that has a diversified portfolio, the leader can expand educational goals and enhance her district, school, or organization.

How to Manage These Stakeholders Effectively

Administrators on a school leadership team should not be micromanaged. The successful educational leader knows that her administrative team is most productive when each individual administrator is in charge of her building, faculty, and programs. In managing this stakeholder group, the team leader's most important responsibility is ensuring that each administrator is supported. Placing the responsibility for success on others provides an avenue for growth and advancement.

BOARD MEMBERS (BOARD OF DIRECTORS)

The elected or appointed officials who are charged with setting the vision for the district while governing its schools are an extremely important stakeholder group that an educational leader must work with throughout his tenure. Even as the chief school administrator (CSA) or superintendent works directly with these individuals on a daily basis, other administrators inside the organizational chart hold roles that somehow affect the needs of the constituents the board members serve. Further, as the board is responsible for the hiring of personnel, the relationship that any administrator fosters with the board can be directly related to job position and job security.

This isn't to insist that the relationship between an administrator and the board needs to be political; however, the educational leader must be politically savvy in dealing with the members charged with the oversight of the school district and the agendas that they may have in consideration of the school community.

How to Manage These Stakeholders Effectively

Managing this stakeholder group can be very tricky. First, interactions between board members and lower-level administrators should be reported to the chief administrator. It is imperative that the school leader tell the superintendent or CSA what the context of the discussion or visit was to maintain transparency among the administrative team and to ensure that no political undermining is taking place. In managing the board, educational leaders must remain consistent in their decision making, communicate with them frequently, and keep them advised on all happenings around the district.

MAYOR, COUNCIL, AND LOCAL ELECTED OFFICIALS

Local officials and political leaders are an important stakeholder group in consideration of an educational system but also a group that isn't always supportive of the work of an educational leader. Including these leaders in the programs, projects, and successes of the district is integral to foster a positive relationship between the district and municipal entities. Positive relations with this group can lead to shared service agreements, program support for citizens, and true fiscal responsibility.

How to Manage These Stakeholders Effectively

It's another sensitive situation, but working with this stakeholder group can be extremely beneficial to the leader and the district he serves. However, the leader must be wholly aware that although the political arenas for both local government officials and the educational community intersect, they are two very different dynamics in consideration of strategies, mission, and their role in the community.

Once again, communication is key to ensuring that this group is aware of any issues that concern the school system and the community as a whole. Local officials should be invited to events and celebrations to show partnership among both government entities and the overall growth in the city or community.

ELECTED STATE OFFICIALS

State officials are outside influencers who can be beneficial in support of programs and funding for a district, school system, or educational organization.

Regardless of political party affiliation, agenda, or platform, these individuals were elected to represent the community, students, and families the educational leader serves. Therefore, these individuals should be included in the interactions, programs, and celebrations of the school community.

How to Manage These Stakeholders Effectively

Communication with these individuals is paramount to an educational leader fostering a positive relationship with this outside stakeholder group. It is also important to note that this communication must not come only in a time of need. Rather, state officials should be part of the progress of the school system as well as be kept abreast of the potential hurdles the district or city schools may face in the near and distant future.

COMMUNITY GROUPS

Other community groups important to any educational system are local and national nonprofit organizations, service agencies, and youth centers. These groups offer support to students and families, sponsor programs and contests, disseminate scholarships, create employment opportunities, and sometimes provide volunteer opportunities for students.

It is important for the educational leader to involve these groups in the schools and interact with them as frequently as possible.

How to Manage These Stakeholders Effectively

The educational leader should include the leaders of these community groups in school functions and when celebrating milestones. Contact includes the head of these organizations and specific officers who deal with scholarship, membership, and other community outreach programs.

BUSINESS OWNERS

Involving the local business community (Rotary, Chamber of Commerce, etc.) allows the educational leader to explore possible partnerships that may lead to internships for students, sponsorships for the district or schools, or assistance with local fund-raising.

How to Manage These Stakeholders Effectively

Meeting with business leaders and individual owners is the best way to foster relationships. The educational leader must be careful to provide equity with local business partnerships, not including one business over another. For example, inviting a local karate school to offer self-defense classes to students when the town has three other karate schools can create a conflict and show inequity or favoritism on the leader's part.

TAXPAYERS

Local taxpayers as stakeholders are typically overlooked by the educational leader. This group is looking for the greatest return on investment, knowing that their taxes support the school system and its related expenses. In districts where communities vote on school budgets, good relations with the taxpayer base are imperative to ensure that the appropriate funding is approved for the smooth, efficient operation of the schools.

How to Manage These Stakeholders Effectively

Getting positive information out into the community about programs, student achievements, and facilities beautification projects is the most important way to gain the support of local taxpayers. This isn't always an easy task, especially when some taxpayers do not have children or family members in the schools.

ALUMNI

An important stakeholder group to consider when making a decision is the alumni of the district or school system. The alumni provide stability for the future of the district, and they can connect to the past as well.

How to Manage These Stakeholders Effectively

The leader should consider an alumni newsletter to keep the stakeholders abreast of the current conditions of the district or happenings among other alumni. Surprisingly, not many districts or PK–12 school systems make it a practice to identify and communicate with alumni on a large scale.

LOCAL REAL ESTATE AGENTS

As a separate stakeholder entity, real estate agents are the individuals who sell the district to new families. Educating these agents on happenings at schools, programs around the district, and upgrades to facilities are the easiest ways to get the positive message out to the broader community.

How to Manage These Stakeholders Effectively

Inviting the agents to plays, programs, sporting events, honors breakfast, and so forth will allow the leader to control the narrative and disseminate information to the community and prospective families in a timely manner. The leader has an important tool—having real estate experts send a positive message about the school community—that can use to her advantage.

RELIGIOUS LEADERS

Religious leaders are very influential in a city or community. It is imperative that the educational leader build a strong relationship with them to gain support for any decisions that may affect their congregations.

Also, it is important for the administrator to meet with each different religious group represented in the school system. This will ensure that all religions are represented, and each leader can discuss the progress of the schools and the district.

How to Manage These Stakeholders Effectively

Along with consistent communication, the educational leader should learn the customs and traditions of each of the religions represented in the school community. What are the important celebration dates? When are the holiest times of the year? Are there any restrictions that families follow? Understanding what the stakeholders value most helps to build a foundation of respect between the educational leader and the leaders of the group.

POLICE AND FIRE OFFICIALS

The relationship with first responders is arguably the most critical one that an educational leader will foster during his tenure in a district or school system. Ensuring transparency and an eagerness to share information with the police and fire chiefs will enable other stakeholder groups, such as parents, to feel comfortable with entrusting the educational leader with the health and safety of their children while in school.

How to Manage These Stakeholders Effectively

Along with an open line of communication with all public safety officials, there must be an understanding among all entities that information must be shared to ensure the safety of students, faculty, and staff in the buildings and throughout the school system. It is also important for the educational leader to encourage onsite and tabletop training with personnel as well as issuing an open invitation for police and fire officials to visit the school campuses as frequently as possible.

YOU MAKE THE CALL!

Joy Luna is an aspiring assistant principal in the Macombs Central School District. Her principal had asked her to research and start a school club to inspire future entrepreneurs. Ms. Luna accepts the challenge and begins to work on the endeavor alongside her staff.

What steps should Ms. Luna take to include the appropriate stakeholders in creating this addition to the school's extracurricular program?

After word gets out about the club, the principal receives a call from the superintendent's office saying that a prominent community member was upset: he has had the same type of program for the youth of the community through his nonprofit organization for the past fifteen years, but the school never wanted to get involved. He also contacted town officials to share his disgust and the lack of respect he was feeling from the school.

How can Ms. Luna rectify the feelings of this important stakeholder?

COACHES' CORNER

1. Describe a time when one of your decisions affected an outside influencer. What ramifications did your decision have? How did you rectify the issue?
2. What are the important stakeholder groups represented in your work or home community? How do these groups influence local everyday decisions?
3. How can a school administrator ensure that he has an appropriate information gateway to all stakeholder groups? Who in the system can the administrator turn to for assistance?

Chapter 11

How to Engage Stakeholder Groups

Chapter 10 outlined stakeholder groups that are an important part of the educational landscape. The educational leader must engage with these stakeholder groups to ensure that she avoids political situations that may arise due to decisions she makes that impact the educational system as a whole and each stakeholder group specifically.

As the educational leader identifies the members of the stakeholder group and understands the best ways to manage each group effectively, she must be able to generate support for her decisions and the actions based on those decisions to continue to make progress and be successful in the district, school, or organization. She understands that regardless of what steps other she will take to gain the highest level of support from these stakeholders, her communication with all members of the community must be succinct, to the point, and always directed toward opportunities for her students and their families.

Further, engagement must also include effective verbal and written communications with all stakeholder groups. Without sending correspondence in a timely manner to members of the community, the leader will not only be subject to the negative perception of being nontransparent, but she also runs the risk of not getting her reasons for the decisions she makes out to the public first.

CONNECT WITH THE STAKEHOLDER LEADERSHIP

As the leader communicates with the stakeholder groups in the district, she must work through the leadership of each individual group to ensure that her message gets to all members unchanged. Further, involving the leader of the group in an immediate fashion will get the message out sooner and empower the stakeholder leader to show support for the decision about to be made.

Some groups may not have an organized leadership hierarchy, so the administrator must use the more influential community members to spread the message she wants to the appropriate people. These groups include alumni, sport parent associations, after-care parents, and other sectors of parents and community members attached to the educational system.

DON'T IGNORE A SITUATION WHEN IT ARISES

The worst possible response to a situation when it arises is to not respond at all. Unfortunately, this is also a way to engage stakeholders quickly because it will negatively impact the progress you have made in the district, school, or organization.

Reaching out to the leadership of a stakeholder group is the quickest, easiest way to disseminate a leadership message to the appropriate channels. Also, many individuals in educational systems cross over into several different stakeholder groups, so the administrator wants to ensure that the message is clear, and the engagement is sustainable.

FOLLOW UP A CORRESPONDENCE WITH A CORRESPONDENCE

To engage stakeholders appropriately, it is imperative that a school leader correspond with them via phone, email, text, or in person. With every correspondence and reply, the leader must send a follow-up memorandum or brief email summarizing what occurred during the meeting and what the next steps will be. The follow-up correspondence is also used to memorialize that a meeting or interaction took place, and it must include a date and time stamp with a copy to an executive secretary or other appropriate position.

ENGAGE STAKEHOLDERS WITHIN TWENTY-FOUR HOURS OF A REQUEST

Although educational administrators are extremely busy, they should return all stakeholder requests within twenty-four hours. This isn't to say that the leader needs to have an answer or a disposition of the problem at that time. Rather, acknowledgment that he has received the questions, comment, or request from a parent or other stakeholder group member is enough to ensure that others know that he is engaged with the community he serves. Also, this gives the school administrator time to investigate the issue more prior to returning the phone call or reaching out to the stakeholder.

USE PERSONAL INTERACTIONS... NOT ALWAYS TECHNOLOGY

For some requests or replies, personal interaction rather than text message or electronic mail is required. This holds true especially if the administrator is dealing with a formal complaint against an employee or a serious child issue that has risen to such a level of concern that it has reached his office.

A follow-up email that outlines what occurred during a meeting, or especially after a phone conference, is appropriate. The correspondence must be written so the tone is not placating in nature or somehow degrading what the parent/stakeholder has discussed. If written in an appropriate, professional manner, the stakeholder will also appreciate the follow-up from the school administrator as a memorialized account of what happened as well.

MAKE COMMUNICATIONS AVAILABLE IN LANGUAGES OTHER THAN ENGLISH

Important school correspondence, fliers, and other notices should all be disseminated in languages most frequently spoken in the district, school, or organization. If a phone call is made, the administrator should have someone interpret for the entire conversation to make the individual feel welcome, unintimidated, and valued. This is important when engaging stakeholders across the educational system.

YOU MAKE THE CALL!

The director of history and humanities for the Conestoga Hills School System just finished a professional development series with his teachers on how to introduce a controversial topic mandated by the federal government to their lesson planning. Although several teachers and staff members feel uneasy about the direction of the curriculum, they reluctantly understand that the director and the school system are just following a legislative directive.

What are the director's next steps in informing stakeholders and preparing for issues related to the new mandate? How should the director assist and support teachers moving forward?

What are some moral, ethical, and legal considerations (MEL) for the director in ensuring that this mandate is implemented in all the appropriate classes?

COACHES' CORNER

1. In educational administration, school leaders are sometimes faced with the challenge of implementing curriculum, policy, and programs that may be controversial or unpopular with certain stakeholder groups and even the administrator himself. Most often, these decisions become political in nature as different groups feel that they should have more control over the direction of instruction and programming in their own communities. Think of a decision or mandate that took place in a district, school, or organization that you are familiar with. What steps did the school administration take to involve stakeholders while ensuring that they were following the mandated guidelines set forth by a higher authority?
2. What steps can an educational leader take to assist teachers and staff members who may be averse to providing instruction for a topic with which they don't agree? What should a leader do if the instructor refuses to comply with the directive?
3. Why is it so important to involve all community stakeholders in the process to lessen the political impact on the administrative decision making?

Chapter 12

The Importance of Feedforward and Feedback Loops

Establishing, using, and perfecting feedforward and feedback loops within constituent groups is an extremely effective tool for school leaders, especially when they are trying to gain buy-in for decisions that affect the school community. The structure and purpose of these loops, along with a school administrator's ability to use each as an integral tool in moving an educational setting forward, is the ultimate way of gauging the amount of support that he has for a particular decision in his district.

The main goal when engaging stakeholders is to gain as much information and insight as possible from them directly related to a program, idea, or event that the administrator is setting forth in the community. This, in turn, provides for a transparent process where each identified group has input into a proposed situation and feels they are a valued part of the decision-making process.

In attempting to gain support, the best administrative tool for the school leader includes a back-and-forth information exchange that occurs in "loops"—brainstormed ideas can be discussed and dissected by members of the group, adding or subtracting what they think will help provide the most positive outcome. This exchange helps the school administrator understand fully where his support lies in considering the decision and allows him to attenuate how he deals with stakeholder groups moving forward.

Within these stakeholder groups, the school leader uses feedback control systems to adjust for what he already understands while feedforward loops hypothesize expected conditions and possible outcomes to adjust what may be involved in setting the perfect conditions. Although most leaders are familiar with feedback, especially dealing with the negative connotations that come along with Monday morning quarterbacks and local gadflies, feedforward is unfamiliar territory for many school leaders.

Simply stated, feedback refers to past actions whereas feedforward provides an action plan for what employees should do in the future. This is a major consideration when dealing with both short- and long-term situations. For a school leader, feedforward from stakeholder groups provides him with added buy-in power for future progress of the district, school, or organization. Feedforward also gives the leader different insight into possible hurdles that he may not have seen coming because he is too close to the situation and dealing more with the feedback that he has attained throughout the process.

Feedback and feedforward both involve the flow of information but serve wholly different purposes. Regardless, the anticipated outcome is the same—to move the system in a positive manner by incorporating as much stakeholder support as possible. Although these terms are used in fields such as engineering, psychology, and business management, educational administration uses these tools in many areas that affect the whole school system.

FEEDBACK

Feedback operates in retrospect or a reactive manner. Gathering feedback means that the leader is asking stakeholders for information about past actions and outcomes that arise from those actions.

In general terms, the purpose of gathering feedback is to evaluate past performance, analyze specific behaviors, or dissect outcomes. Most importantly, the school leader should insist that feedback includes suggestions and ideas to improve the condition being discussed or provide support to ensure success moving forward.

FEEDFORWARD

Feedforward operates in a proactive manner or is prospective. Here, stakeholders and individuals use evidence or historical data trends to provide guidance or information before an action takes place or a decision is made.

The sole purpose of feedforward is for school leaders to gain information in anticipation of future events, actions, or potential outcomes. Stakeholders who provide strong feedforward loops feel confident that they have given guidance and direction toward successful implementation of a future goal or condition. This becomes extremely important to stakeholder groups that may be linked directly to the outcomes of the proposed action.

Both feedback and feedforward loops are valuable to the school leader and the development and improvement of his district, school, or organization. By using these loops, the leader can gain a knowledge base around the current and proposed actions while providing a platform for stakeholders to feel that their buy-in is important to the direction of the system.

PROVIDING LOOPS TO ENGAGED STAKEHOLDERS

In previous chapters we have discussed the makeup of stakeholder groups and how a school leader can engage herself with group members. Once this has been established, the next step in the process is to provide these group members with the ability to formulate feedback and feedforward responses to the issues that the leader has proposed.

It is important that the leader understand that feedback and feedforward loops should only be considered influential if they are received by groups of stakeholders who are organized and interact with one another on separate occasions. This includes parent-teacher organizations, community forums sponsored by a superintendent of schools or other school administrator, sports associations, alumni groups, and so forth. What it shouldn't include is feedback from rogue individuals using specific conditions to diminish the leadership role of the administrator, embarrass her in some manner, or give the school district or organization a black eye. For those individuals, most feedback gained includes a specific agenda that is one-sided and benefits finger pointing to persuade others away from supporting the decisions of the school leader.

Rather, getting stakeholders together to discuss what has already occurred and/or what possible future scenarios may entail is critical in ensuring that the leader gains the most support possible for his decisions that will impact the educational system. Using the directed informational leadership approach discussed earlier, the administrator should provide appropriate, leading questions so that she can fully understand what stakeholder members are providing.

The directed informational approach is important in this case because the leader can ensure that the information she is obtaining aligns with the question or concerns at hand and the discussions do not veer to a tangent that may lead to outside discussions or other problems. Even though a school leader is constantly dealing with a plethora of issues, stakeholder input in a feedback/feedforward format will only be beneficial and productive if the stakeholders and district leadership are homing in on a specific topic. Moving away from the issue at hand decreases potential buy-in from stakeholders for the decision in question.

By controlling the narrative and the dialogue set forth by the conditions inside the stakeholder group or committee, the leader can ensure that her questions both guide the loops and include follow-up questions to elicit responses that also relate to support for the program, event, or decision to be made. Any feedback she obtains can be used to determine corrections or additions she needs to make to show that she has used stakeholder support.

Ideas presented to the leader as feedforward could easily be used to strengthen her relationship with the group and enhance the value the stakeholders feel by becoming more widely involved in the process. Further, feedforward may produce different pathways to progress that she hadn't considered or identify outliers who may hinder progress.

In each situation, the leader must be fully engaged with the stakeholders to ensure that she facilitates the discussions to generate the most favorable outcome when gaining support through stakeholder data. Using feedback and feedforward loops can increased support for the school leader, making group members feel tied into the progress and decision-making process of the leadership team. From there, members of the group will push the message out to other stakeholders and community members and will take responsibility for the decisions that are occurring because they were involved in formulating them.

YOU MAKE THE CALL!

Margaret Fusco is president of the local teacher's union and has been an employee in the Rock Valley Public Schools District for twenty-five years. She has seen the district transition through several superintendents and numerous administrators over her tenure and has worked alongside the administrative team on many of the district initiatives still in place today.

As assistant principal in charge of activities, you were asked by the school business administrator to review programs that could be eliminated to save money in the upcoming budget. The district faces a financial burden: state aid figures were not as expected, the costs of benefits are rising, and the needs of special education students are increasing.

Upon reviewing the data for the programs at the school, you identify three that are not providing the high return on investment that they did when they were implemented five years before you came to the district. You discuss your findings with your building principal, who immediately suggests that you include Ms. Fusco in your discussions.

Why did the principal offer this suggestion before you discuss your findings with the business administrator who charged you with the task?

Do you think that speaking with Ms. Fusco is an appropriate next step? If so, how would you approach the topic?

COACHES' CORNER

1. It is imperative that an educational leader learns the history behind past decisions made in a district, school, or organization to ensure that she wholly understands the time, work, and effort afforded to that decision by past and current stakeholders. Without knowing the historical context of a program or event, for example, that a new decision may attenuate or even eliminate, the administrator can create a multitude of problems and invoke an unnecessary and unwanted political process. Think of a decision that was made to eliminate a program or initiative in a school or district with which you are familiar. What were the implications of such a decision on the stakeholders?
2. How did local politics affect the decision?
3. Why is it important for an educational leader to identify the stakeholders and members of his team involved in a project or initiative at its onset?

Chapter 13

Gadflies

Every community has gadflies, and every public board, council, or entity must humor them at meetings while they exercise their right to free speech even if it is only transmitted in half-truths, misinformation, and a message out of context.

By definition, a gadfly persistently provokes or annoys others with criticism, schemes, ideas, demands, and requests. In the public arena, many individuals see gadflies as entertaining, and many find them to be an important system of checks and balances to keep local politicians and school administrators in line when they make decisions that affect the district's instruction and programs, financial responsibility, personnel, governance, and operations.

At least in the field of educational administration, stakeholders and other members of the community will ask questions periodically to get information, complain about a specific situation at the schools, offer ideas to enhance the district, or complain about you and your decisions as a leader of the school, district, or organization. Most often, these complaints are in public forums or social media, and stakeholders can be very terse and unfriendly at times. This type of criticism comes with the territory. This is why school administrators need to grow a thick skin when they cross over from the classroom to administration. The once-beloved classroom teacher easily becomes the "suit" who only makes 50 percent of her constituents happy with each decision she makes.

By not taking the rhetoric personally, the leader can move forward using the comments and complaints to her advantage. She can easily become aware of the key players/stakeholders in the community whose message she should value and who is only a gadfly, constantly looking to wreak havoc on the educational system and the school administrator's career.

Stakeholders who are genuinely criticizing or just dislike the school administrator should be taken very seriously. Most often, these individuals are respected members of the community, and they are somehow entrenched in community programs and local political circles. Any answers that a leader provides these individuals must be backed with evidence because, most often, follow-up questions will be used to move a point forward or strengthen their position in the community.

Ignoring these individuals or not providing a strong, concrete answer to their inquiries will only bring more attention to the situation at hand and may even cause more individuals to become involved in the situation. Not only will the leader's inability—or refusal—to answer create an unnecessary dialogue among members in the community, but treating specific members of the community in a certain way may be seen as abhorrent behavior. This, in turn, may cause the school leader to lose the support of different stakeholders and put decisions, programs, and plans in jeopardy for little or no apparent reason.

Conversely, a gadfly has a platform that includes specific conditions and protocols where it is apparent that no answer and no solution would be acceptable to end the reported problems. As parents and other stakeholder members with genuine concerns will link the conditions and issues to ensure that the school administrator finds a pathway to solve the problem, the gadfly seems to present unrelated, usually irrelevant issues. Be aware of this very important distinction, understanding who within the community you serve may be a concerned stakeholder and who may only be an individual who creates chaos so he can be considered the I-told-you-so community member.

Thus, identifying and understanding the gadfly is integral to consistently keeping one move ahead of him, always being prepared for collateral damage that may stem from an open public records request or information obtained from another public records source. Once again, this is an important concept for the educational leader; any stumble or inability to address issues that come from the gadfly can dampen progress the leader has made and ultimately irreparably harm the school leader's reputation and career. Further, being unprepared for what comes from a chaotic, possibly heated exchange can negatively affect support for decisions the leader needs to make for her students and the school community.

Usually, educational gadflies repeat themselves by restating the same complaints or concerns at each meeting. Unfortunately, the school administrator cannot ignore these advances even once because that instance may be misconstrued that the leader doesn't know the answer. Instead, the leader needs to reiterate a consistent answer each time.

If the leader isn't truly sure of the answer, then she must explain that she needs more time to investigate the concern and provide an answer at the next public opportunity. That way she remains transparent and ensures that everyone hears the answer the way she wants to produce it in a public forum. The worst possible scenario is to provide incorrect information, or not provide an answer at all.

A leader who ignores the gadflies in his community will face a long, uphill battle, always trying to understand what political angle the individual is using to catch the school administrator or members of his team.

YOU MAKE THE CALL!

Ms. Shelly Frey is the former parent-teacher organization president of the Clearwater School District and is still an active and outspoken community member who regularly attends school board meetings. As the superintendent of schools, you have had several interactions with Ms. Frey during your tenure in the district, some pleasant and some not so pleasant.

During the public portion of the February meeting of the board of education, Ms. Frey approached the podium and began to discuss something she had heard from other community members regarding a situation that occurred involving you and several other members of the administration at a local restaurant during a holiday party in December. Ms. Frey had pictures on her phone and described accounts of the administrative team possibly acting lewdly toward other patrons and being obnoxious, which you were allowing to happen. Although she admits that this was after work hours on your own time, many families frequent the restaurant, and she feels that you should hold yourself to a higher standard as the face of the district and role model to the district's children.

What is your next move as the superintendent of schools? Consider all stakeholder groups that you would need to report to to explain the alleged actions that Ms. Frey described. Should you be concerned?

COACHES' CORNER

1. Educational leaders are held to a higher standard in interactions with community members and stakeholders outside the school day. When leaders act irresponsibly or embarrassingly, the public perceives this as a sign of weakness or an inability to lead in an appropriate manner. This includes interactions with stakeholders, actions that occur in the administrator's hometown, financial considerations, and stories or situations (personal and professional) from the past that are memorialized on social media. Think of a situation where an administrator was in

the media or was questioned at a public meeting regarding a personal situation, problem, or allegation? How did the administrator handle the issue?
2. Every district, school, or organization has gadflies. Discuss strategies or best practices that an administrator can use to help ensure that the actions of these individuals and the political agenda behind their actions do not affect the local decisions that need to be made throughout the educational system.
3. Is it more or less beneficial to the educational leader to include these individuals early in the decision-making process?

Chapter 14

How to Spot Political Machines

Educational leaders get into unfavorable circumstances when they cannot pinpoint the political trends and players in their community or organization. Although much of this is innate, certain methods and protocols can be used to determine the political entities who influence decision-making practices.

REAL OR JUST LOOKS REAL

An educational leader must use his influence to help ensure that he gains support for the decisions he makes for himself and the greater good of his students and school community. Throughout his tenure in the district, the leader will identify individuals who are influential political players and individuals others will identify as part of the political machine attached to the educational community.

Although it may take time and a little bit of research on the administrator's part, he must decide which operatives carry weight in consideration of the educational system and which just act like they do.

Simply stated, rhetoric and the politically uneducated involvement of local citizens tend to make certain individuals in a city or community appear more intelligent, powerful, and overly connected to the decisions of a government agency than they are. In fact, many former political activists, who may have held elected positions or were gadflies during earlier political campaigns, are thought to have the same political prowess and influence many years later only because they were involved in the past and are perceived to have maintained their political stature through time.

The only way an educational leader can break this cycle of unwarranted influence is by identifying the true members of the political machine and dismissing the others. The leader must have the confidence to ask the right questions to be sure which individuals still hold influence over the decisions that she will make that impact her district school or organization. These questions include inquiring into which outside organizations the perceived influencer belongs to or with whom the outside political influencer aligns.

SEVENTH TIME'S THE CHARM!

A very interesting consideration in the local political arena deals with the notion that any individual who runs as a candidate for a seat on the board of education or other municipal elected office will ultimately win a seat if she continues to run. Although the cliché "practice makes perfect" may come to mind, or the victory will stem from name recognition, the reality is that one election cycle will just include the perfect storm of factors for the candidate to get elected.

Why is this important for an administrator to know? Political machines run slates of candidates every election to attain the most viable win percentage for any candidate because all candidates most likely will follow the agenda set by the political boss. Thus, a candidate who was a former official or someone who doesn't seem to the educational administrator to have any political influence may one day be representing the community.

The educational leader must always keep this possibility in mind, knowing that one-time political allies who may have turned against her at some point can one day again be in the forefront of political influence in the district or community. Sure, it may take seven, eight, or ten elections before their return, but the political machine will always rear its ugly head when the opportunity arises.

This type of opportunity usually comes during a transition of power in the educational system, or when the system is facing a crisis, and the machine controls the narrative to win majority power over the governing body.

IDENTIFYING THE RIGHT ADVISERS

Educational leaders surround themselves with strong allies who help them lead, manage, and operate their district, school, or organization. When navigating the political landscape of any educational system, it is important that the administrator interacts with competent advisers to help him make important decisions that will effect change throughout the environment.

Much of his counsel will represent the various academic and financial needs of the system. But fostering a relationship with stakeholders entrusted with identifying and advising the leader on the political operatives and the related machines in the city or community is important to the longevity of the school leader in his administrative role.

To echo the previous chapters, it is exceedingly important that the educational leader stay politically savvy, not political. The right advisers can not only identify the major political players in your circle but act as buffers for the administrator in dealing with political adversaries and any decisions that need to be made that can influence change in the system.

YOU MAKE THE CALL!

Sonny Carisi is a local detective and star quarterback for the Lyndenwood High School State Championship squad of 1982. Over the past twenty-five years, Sonny has worked as campaign manager for many local town officials elected to political leadership roles in Lyndenwood.

Your second week as Lyndenwood High School principal, several coaches and faculty members are discussing the upcoming school year and advising you about parts of the "landscape" of the school system. You are intrigued by stories you hear and connections you learn about, but you are very optimistic that you can make your own decisions about certain individuals as the school year moves forward.

As the summer ends, you have lunch at the Dawghouse eatery in the center of town. As you enter the restaurant, you are immediately greeted by Detective Carisi, who is just finishing his meal.

"So, you're the new sheriff in town, hey? They call me Sonny."

You recognize him from the pictures and accolades around the high school, his face and physique nearly unchanged all these years later.

"Oh, yes, sir. Hello. It's very nice to meet you."

Sonny continues the conversation, using his detective skills to ask how your summer went and if you filled all the positions left vacant by the principal you replaced.

"He was a joke," Sonny explains. "Worst thing that's ever happened to Lyndenwood."

Sonny continues as you start to look at the takeout menu.

"Hey, listen, someone gave me a résumé that might be helpful if you still have positions to fill. You mind if I drop it off later?"

As principal of Lyndenwood and the newest member of the administrative team, how do you handle this situation? What are your next steps, and who do you tell about your encounter with Detective Carisi?

Chapter 14

COACHES' CORNER

1. Every district or educational system contends with local political activists who either attempt to or do control the educational landscape. It is imperative that an educational leader identify these political machines and the key players to be prepared for the inevitable interactions that he will face. Think about an important political figure in a school district. How should an administrator approach and interact with such an individual apropos of the moral, ethical, and legal (MEL) considerations that surround local decisions?
2. What are several ways that administrators can assist faculty and staff members to avoid contact with political forces?
3. Detail pros and cons when it comes to relationships with political operatives and prominent figures in the community.

Chapter 15

Surveying and Surviving Political Trends

As a follow-up to earlier chapters that described an educational leader's roles and responsibilities for navigating the political landscape, this chapter outlines political tells, the steps that an educational leader can take to foresee future political changes both inside and outside an organization, and how to remain influential during the political ebb and flow of an educational system or institution. The ability to understand, identify, and then use specific intuitive tools to survey and outlast trending political views and the decisions tied to those views can enhance and extend the tenure of the school leader in his district or building.

Although a leader must know when she is causing the politics of her office to trend and others to react to the decisions she makes. Along those lines, the leader must be cautious when undeniable actions begin to take place on a frequent and consistent basis.

In all, when the educational leader pinpoints the changing political trends every time (not just the first time) things of this nature arise, she is better suited to address and manage both the situation at hand and, most importantly, the individual or group creating the drama surrounding the issue in the first place. It is also important that the educational leader recognize that even though she may have identified the cause and the players, it may not be the best time to act on the situation or topic. Rather, it may be in her best interest to identify and monitor the trending political pattern, see how it affects her decision-making abilities and political capital in the system, and be prepared to act when—or if—the time is right.

AN INABILITY TO MEET

When members of the identified political machine, municipal or city government, or from the educational leader's administrative team suddenly can't meet with her or can't find time for her in their schedule, it appears to be a political trend to avoid her, to box her out, to sever ties, or to avoid compromise.

When this occurs and the school leader feels the time is optimal to manage the trend so she controls the narrative, she should publicly call out the individual and offer a specific meeting date and time to discuss the issue. Placing the onus on the individual refusing to meet with the school administrator, especially if it is expressed in a public forum, will at least create a formal record. It shows that the leader is doing all she can to rectify a situation or get in front of a potential issue that may create future problems for the district or the community.

It is important that the school leader not ignore the unwillingness to meet coming from the outside influencer or stakeholder group. If she ignores the lack of cooperation by the other entity, the perception one day will be that she didn't do enough on her end to try to make the situation work.

TABLE FOR TWO? ... OR THREE?

When a meeting does occur, is it between the leader and the stakeholder, or should another individual mediate? Sometimes having a neutral party present is a plus for the school administrator and can work in his favor. However, when someone comes to a meeting unannounced to discuss issues that may only be between the administrator and the other party, that is somewhat concerning.

If this should occur, the educational leader must calmly decide whether to hold the meeting or reschedule at another time. The main consideration here is making sure that the stakeholder doesn't know whether the administrator feels threatened or just doesn't care to discuss the situation with anyone but the stakeholder herself.

NO ONE IS SPEAKING AFTER YOU SPEAK

Suppose no one speaks up to back you up. This cue is a little harder to detect, but once it is acknowledged, it definitely is a telltale sign that you are losing your ability to survive the political trends on the horizon. When the educational leader delivers a speech, discusses a new program, or advocates for something for his students and the district, a line of individuals should follow him to the podium to support the cause. The moment the leader pours out her heart and no one speaks after her is the moment that the leader understands her net worth. This is even more apparent when your building principal (if you are an assistant principal) or your board president (if you are a superintendent, business administrator, etc.), doesn't reiterate what you just said or wrote before a meeting, crisis situation, or other process issue.

LESS QUESTIONS . . . MORE COMMENTS

When the gadflies, parents, and other stakeholders approach the educational leader and pose questions, they are perceived as engaged learners whether they spark interesting conversation or make comments to try to trick a leader into giving them more information. Regardless, the conversation itself shows interest in the leader and what he is doing to impact the school system. As mentioned, it may be positive feedback, or it may be a negative question that can be used time by the stakeholder to cast a shadow on the administration and its programs.

Once the questions stop being asked, it shows a lack of interest in the work of the educational leader and the change occurring throughout the system. One may argue that a quiet board meeting or an open forum with no comments indicates a well-run system with few issues and problems. To the contrary, a system that has limited opposition to the major players or minimal to no checks and balances for all that has been accomplished is a school system where no one is interested in its mission and no one has checked instruction and program in the district to ensure that it is meeting and surpassing all standards.

FINDING OUT AFTER AND NOT BEFORE

One key way that an educational leader pinpoints when he is moving away from surviving political trends is when he learns about an occurrence after others find out instead of before the action makes its way outside the system. Colleagues and subordinates who respect the leader's position of oversight and control in the district or school will try to protect him from embarrassment or unnecessary turmoil by giving him information directly when—or immediately following—an incident.

When the leader is dismissed by his team, and the team takes less interest in the fact that his knowledge of a situation should be paramount, then the leader must realize that he has lost some control over the team. Sporadic failure of members to inform the leader of an incident does not means that a coup is forming; however, a seasoned educational leader should be able to ascertain which team members still support him and which don't.

DECISIONS WITHOUT PRIOR KNOWLEDGE

One key tell that an educational administrator is losing to a political trend is when team members or stakeholders make decisions on important programs, projects, or concepts without informing the leader. Many key decisions made in a district, school, or organization include stakeholder input and feedback from the current administration. Therefore, the educational leader absolutely must be informed of any decision before it is made and presented to the community.

Decisions made without direction from the educational leader not only create a dismissive environment, where the leader looks put off or less valuable, but they also shift power to the individual making the decision and cause others in the organization to lose some respect for the leader and be made, at some point, to choose a side.

YOU MAKE THE CALL!

Michael Ernest Lowman is in his first term as mayor of Elmwood Village and has promised the citizens that he will work with school leaders to expand the city's schools to combat the growing enrollment and overcrowding concerns stemming from an influx of families. As the chief education officer in the district, you met with the mayor right after his election to discuss the state of the educational system, test scores, and aging school facilities that are well beyond capacity.

In the first year of his term, the mayor worked with his political allies to help the city schools move forward, supporting programs and initiatives to navigate some of the hurdles that you as the school chief continue to identify. On the surface your relationship seems to be strong, but the reality is that he is both jealous of the influence you have over the city and angry that you don't ask his permission before you make a decision.

Over the next several years, you continue to grow more influential in the city while his support begins to wane. You recognize that he is no longer involved in the happenings around the schools, and he is becoming more critical of your decisions and the faculty and staff members you are hiring.

Noticing a change in your professional relationship, you attempt to set up a few meetings with him, but he is unresponsive. It becomes obvious to you that there is a new political trend in the city, a trend in which you will play no part.

What next steps can you take as educational leader in the district? What potential issues can occur when a relationship of this nature no longer exists?

COACHES' CORNER

1. The relationship that educational leaders have with local political operatives can change based on strategic differences, miscommunication, or a shift in power. Leaders must be aware of changing trends in the political landscape and how they can affect their ability to lead effectively. Describe a situation where you have witnessed a strong relationship between two political figures become weakened. What factors caused this to occur? Could it have been avoided?
2. What compromises must occur when attempting to mend differences between two strong leaders for the greater good of the community?
3. What is the possible fallout from political turmoil between leaders within a school system? Between leaders inside and outside the school system?

Chapter 16

The Playbook of Politics for Educational Leaders

Every great coach has a playbook filled with plays that she will use to gain and secure the advantage over an opponent. Throughout the course of a game or contest, the coach also has several key go-to plays that are the foundation of her team, and she always knows she can use these plays when she needs a positive outcome.

This chapter includes different influencers that an educational leader can use to ensure that politics stays in line with the decision-making process. These are the set plays that the educational leader can use when he needs to gain momentum, secure power, or win in a strategic setting.

This obviously doesn't include every possible play that could be included in this type of playbook, and not every play will work for every educational leader. Regardless, each educational leader must have a set of actions he can take to mobilize the members of his team to ensure that he can navigate the local politics and the political trends that he faces every day.

STUDY AN OPPONENT'S WEAKNESSES . . . AND KNOW WHEN TO USE THEM AGAINST HIM

Sun Tzu said, "Appear weak when you are strong, and strong when you are weak." It is imperative for anyone preparing to go into battle to wholly understand the strengths and weaknesses of his opponent. Focusing on an opponent's strengths is an important way to defend oneself against aggression or to overthrow the leader or weaken his ability to lead others. However, it is just as important for the educational leader to study an opponent's weaknesses so that he knows how and when to strike hardest to win a battle.

The second step in this process is for the educational leader to know when to use his strengths against an opponent's weaknesses. The administrator must ensure that he doesn't act too soon, too late, or not at all. Although much of this comes with experience, the leader must take into consideration the individual he is working against and his connection to the situation at hand and the educational system as a whole.

BE NICE UNTIL IT'S TIME NOT TO BE NICE

No one wants to work with a manager or boss who is unpleasant, patronizing, or just not nice. The educational leader must ensure that her persona is pleasant and supportive of her workforce all the time. When this is the case, productivity is at its greatest, and the morale of the team leads to greater productivity and accomplishments.

It is also important for the leader to be stern when it is absolutely necessary. This will prove to others that she is holding her employees accountable and moving the school, district, or organization forward. Also, it is important that her workers know that although she is personable and caring of her team, her kindness should not be viewed as weakness. Rather, her tightening the reins when and only when it is necessary will gain more respect from her workers; it will mean more when it is relevant to the situation, not unwarranted.

BELIEVE THE UNBELIEVABLE

"There's no way he said that about me." Or "I can't believe that Johnny overheard Ms. Bell say she doesn't like the program." Well, believe it. Whatever you think someone won't say about you, your programs, or the decisions you make surely will be said at some point during your career. And if, for some unexplained reason, you never have something similar said to you, then you aren't challenging or pushing your people enough.

In the field of educational administration, the unimaginable happens every day. Students, faculty, and staff consistently surprise one another with actions and ideas that can either be completely expected or the administrator had no idea what to expect. Instead of losing time trying to figure out the why, it is more valuable way to use the time to determine the what and the how.

REVENGE IS A DISH BEST SERVED COLD . . . OR NOT AT ALL

A normal reaction is for an individual to want to strike back when he is attacked. Whether it is connected to someone who is close or a true adversary, it is imperative that the educational leader stay calm, focused, and take a breath before acting in revenge.

DON'T MAKE THE SAME MISTAKE ONCE

As a young education leader, I had a framed sign hanging on the wall that read, "I am not responsible . . . but I am to blame." With a plethora of incidents occurring throughout the day, it is absolutely impossible for an administrator to take care of every situation at a minute's notice.

However, there definitely are times when something just doesn't seem right, or a red flag has made its way into the administrator's decision-making process. If something doesn't seem right—it probably isn't. Thus, the school leader must use his instinct and stop any decision or approval that isn't the perfect fit.

THE BOB AND WEAVE

Sometimes, the educational leader may just not be ready to decide or act on a particular situation. When this is the case, the administrator must pause the process to provide more time to research the question or request.

It is also important that the administrator place the onus on the other party when looking to extend the time frame. By asking the individual to answer follow-up questions or to assist with researching alternate answers/choices, the leader brings less attention to the fact that he is causing the delay.

CREATE CHAOS

If the educational leader really wants to see how something is affecting his team or if he needs to flesh out the real story, he must consider creating chaotic, uncomfortable situations for individuals. This type of environment brings out the best in individuals as they try to solve problems and use mediation skills to work out an issue through a process. Here, the administrator fosters competition among his team, which also keeps the climate fresh as long as it is monitored.

A great example of this is when two or more subordinates cannot find a solution to a situation and they ask the leader for assistance. Through directed informational leadership the administrator can ensure that the decision he wants will come from the discussion, but he should continually push the discussion back on the sparring subordinates until they work out the issue. This type of chaos allows the leader to ensure that he is continually creating an autonomous environment as well as forcing those subordinates to work together and compromise or agree to disagree to move the district forward.

YOU MAKE THE CALL!

You are the director of curriculum and instruction in a PK–12 district, and you work closely with three department supervisors under your leadership. Last week, you tasked them to choose new program software for remedial work in the elementary grades, but the supervisors cannot come to a consensus on which software package is best suited for those students.

One supervisor, Johnny Gobba, came to your office and explained that they couldn't reach an agreement and they needed your assistance. As the supervisors never worked well together, you saw this project as an opportunity to have them gain mutual respect for one another through finding a common outcome.

When you asked Johnny to tell the others to work it out, and he left your office in a flippant manner.

What are your next steps in assisting the supervisors both to work through their differences and make the correct programmatic decision? What challenges do you face as the administrator in charge?

COACHES' CORNER

1. Educational leaders have their own ways of dealing with specific situations that will help lead to support for local decisions. What are some ways you would deal with employees who are not getting along with one another or who cannot work together in a productive manner?
2. Do you think that an educational leader should get involved in confrontations between subordinates early or later in the mediation process?
3. Describe how you have used one of the plays outlined in chapter 16 during your workday. What challenges are associated with using some of these methods?

Chapter 17

The Importance of Protecting Others

Educational leaders work every day to ensure that students, faculty, and staff members receive the supplies, programs, and support they need to be successful throughout the school day. Besides the constant balancing act that school administrators perform in consideration of instruction and program; fiscal accountability; governance; operations; and managing personnel, the political landscape continues to change as the years progress, new families become more involved in the school community, and local and national trends tend to affect the values that parents have established for their children.

To complete both his daily and overall mission of running his school, district, or organization effectively and efficiently to show progress, the educational leader must understand how local politics influence decisions in the educational system and how those decisions ultimately affect the people that he surrounds himself with to ensure that change occurs. Thus, it is important that the leader understands those individuals who are important to his cause and who will help him continue to move the needle north every year to show growth and prosperity from the programs that he has initiated and continues to run for his students and their success.

Simply put, individuals who feel safe and protected will not only perform better but will reciprocate the same protections for the leader. Influential teachers, colleague administrators, and staff members will both spread the word that the leader is doing his best for the school and families and show major support for the administrator when he faces criticism or backlash on social media from an unpopular decision.

In times of uncertainty and crisis, it is extremely important that the educational leader shows those individuals he serves that they have his unwavering support. This holds even more true when the political landscape changes, mandates are enforced, and social paradigms shift to advance a change in curriculum and program structure. A true leader doesn't let his team members become the brunt of opposition; rather, he is in the forefront protecting his allies and sorting out necessary changes or compromises to ensure that progress continues.

YOU MAKE THE CALL!

Olivia Calindriello has been teaching music for seventeen years at Rhoades Elementary School, and she has always been your biggest supporter. As assistant principal, you are in charge of daily dismissal, and Mrs. Calindriello was the first teacher to volunteer for that duty when you came to the district eight years ago.

Yesterday, you received a message that the mother of a third-grade student, Caesar Egan, wanted to discuss something that occurred in music class that afternoon. During your lunch break, you reached out to Ms. Egan to see how you could help.

Ms. Egan was irate. She went on to explain that her son Caesar told her that during yesterday's music class, Mrs. Calindriello began to discuss the upcoming election and how she hoped that all the parents would vote for someone new or the trip to the zoo may be canceled.

Ms. Egan went on to explain that Mrs. Calindriello has done things like this before, but she never said anything out of fear of retaliation against her son. The rumor from the PTO parents is that Mrs. Calindriello doesn't like it when parents complain about her, and she ignores students in class if their parents have issues with her teaching.

You are taken aback by the allegations that you heard from Ms. Egan. You have never had any complaints or negative calls about Ms. Calindriello, and you have grown to know her style and demeanor working closely with her over the past eight years.

This seems more like a misunderstanding or a miscommunication.

What are your next steps as assistant principal? Besides the steps you need to take regarding the investigation, what else must be done in anticipation that this story will get out on social media?

COACHES' CORNER

1. Educational leaders are charged with ensuring that complaints are investigated and handled accordingly. Although some complaints are reported accurately, at times students misinterpret comments or mistakes by faculty and staff. It is important that the leader mediates any

miscommunication, that she ensures that any discrepancies are corrected and contained so as not to spread further rumors or exaggerate events. Discuss a time when something you said or did was or could have been misunderstood by students or others. When did you realize that a miscommunication had taken place? How did you correct the situation?
2. Why is it important for a school administrator to thoroughly investigate complaints to protect faculty and staff from rumors and social media rhetoric?
3. Discuss some strategies for dealing with social media campaigns that share stories in which only part of the true story is revealed.

Chapter 18

Transparency 101

Transparency is a term that administrators often use and individuals who may not see eye to eye with the educational leader usually challenge. Being and remaining transparent is an important tool in building the political and human capital needed to influence decisions in any school system or educational organization. The school leader must be careful not to use her transparent style so it looks like she is placating stakeholders and community members. In other words, whatever she uses to ensure a transparent process or transparent dialogue between the administrator and others must be genuine and viewed as her ability to provide a true picture of what has occurred and what is expected.

It is most important that the school administrator not come across as fake when delivering a message that is transparent. This can be avoided if he is prepared for questions that may arise out of the discussion and ensures that the information being shared is relevant. In any case, offering the full, transparent story includes incorporating different elements into the discussion that lend itself to the final disposition best suited for both the educational system and the administrator.

An educational leader needs several different levels of transparency to be successful in her position. At any given time during a discussion or presentation of the topic, any one of the levels may come to the forefront to ensure that stakeholders are guided appropriately and consistently.

LEVEL 1—AUDIENCE

Choosing the correct audience to address the issue to is an immediate need when considering the most transparent process and stakeholder buy-in to any situation that the educational leader faces. It is imperative that the appropriate groups are part of this process in which each stakeholder can provide feedback and feedforward after listening to the administrator provide the background and plans surrounding the situation.

LEVEL 2—PROS AND CONS

A second area of transparency for an educational leader to include are the pros and cons that surround the process and the decision being proposed. The leader must explain to the stakeholders all the potential impacts of the outcomes so that members of the community will not be surprised when any impact is announced after the decision is implemented.

In this case, the administrator gives community members and others the opportunity to understand what comes along with the potential pluses or drawbacks, and she receives input from the stakeholders that may give her insight into the decision that she needs to make to enhance the educational system.

LEVEL 3—HISTORICAL CONTEXT

Being transparent includes providing a historical context for the entire community before a decision is made. This lets individuals understand and compare where we were before, where we are now, and where we are heading. Providing the history of the process goes a long way provided that the administrator is transparent and open about what it took to get to where he is now and who else was involved along the journey. This also helps take away any political optics from the administrator's decision because the pathway to it includes the history of the entire issue and what was previously done to get to the appropriate decision.

LEVEL 4—RESEARCH AND DATA TRENDS

Completing research on the discussion topic leading to the decision is an important way to include direct evidence about why the educational leader is making that decision. The research should include both support for the decision and even information that may oppose or provide an alternative to the decision being suggested. This provides an extremely transparent view of what the administrator feels is necessary for the continued progress of the district, school, or organization.

LEVEL 5—INCORPORATING IDEAS

The strongest form of transparency occurs when the administrator incorporates the ideas and feedback/feedforward from members of all stakeholder groups into the decision-making process and the proposed action plan. In doing this, the leader proves to the community and constituent base that he is transparent in his decision-making process: he has taken the ideas and suggestions provided and incorporated them into his plan of action. Although the ideas may be directed by the leader (meaning that not every idea will become part of the action plan that will lead to a decision), using what was collected shows concern by the leader and his team.

YOU MAKE THE CALL!

Dr. Elliot Cronk, director of research and data for the Spring Valley Schools, is preparing to present the annual assessment report to the school community. It will feature scores from last spring, include a longitudinal comparison of aggregate rankings over the past five years, and will outline an action plan to help enhance student scores.

Dr. Cronk sent the data presentation to the board office for approval, and he heard back from the chief of staff several hours before the public meeting with the community.

"Elliot, we think that maybe you can leave out that fifth-grade math number that dipped pretty low," the chief said. "We have a pretty big election year ahead of us, and I don't want to give the other side anything to use against us."

Dr. Cronk explained to the chief that the fifth-grade assessment had several unexpected challenges, and he could explain it to the community.

"Well, I guess it's ultimately your call," the chief added reluctantly. "I'm just telling you the orders I was given."

What advice would you give Dr. Cronk as he faces this dilemma? How should he move forward?

COACHES' CORNER

1. Educational leaders are often faced with making decisions in which the outcome has political ramifications. A leader must be cognizant of how the decisions she makes and the types of information she shares may affect both her and others. Although this information may not sway her reaction or decision, at least she will be aware of the possible fallout

from the decisions she makes. Discuss a time when you were asked to attenuate, modify, or leave out something to control the narrative. How did you handle the situation? What steps did you follow to make your decision?
2. Use the MEL paradigm to outline the necessary considerations in the chapter 18 scenario.
3. What are the political and employment ramifications if Dr. Cronk refuses to take the advice of the chief of staff? What are the ramifications if Dr. Cronk follows the suggestions offered?

Chapter 19

Et tu, Brute?

A successful leader knows that the only way to create and sustain a strong, healthy organization is to have a leadership team that contains progressive individuals who want to grow the company or organization while exponentially enhancing their own career through any viable means.

Commonly known as cutting someone's legs out from under him, a strong leader can identify and defend against members from his own team who actively work to get him out of his position. Although it seems like thwarting such opposition is easy in most cases, the reality is that the leader cannot lose sight of his mission and must make decisions based on his need to protect himself from an underling who is working to take his job.

This isn't completely a bad thing. On the surface, the idea of an individual doing all she can to make it look like she's better than the current leader fosters healthy competition and bolsters creativity. Further, the leader of any organization or department should only want others working for her who aspire to sit in her seat one day.

Attempting to take a leader's position from him is not uncommon in educational administration. Fear of this happening combined with local political influencers can impact decisions the school leader makes to protect the programs he has established, the personnel he's hired, the positions he's created, and—ultimately—his career.

In Shakespeare's tragedy *Julius Caesar*, a dying Caesar exclaims, "Et tu, Brute?" (And you, Brutus?) on seeing his friend Marcus Brutus among his assassins. In the play, Caesar, the ruler and most powerful man in Rome, is assassinated by political rivals including his best friend and confidant, Brutus. The phrase is used to describe when someone a leader trusts joins others who betray or dismiss him. Although Brutus joins assassinating Caesar, he does not do it out of personal hatred but for political gain and thinking that Caesar's death was for the greater good of Rome.

The same holds true in educational administration. The closest members of the leader's team or cabinet may look to diminish the leader's power by delivering a crushing blow to his political status or power base when the opportunity arises. Because it is the natural order of the administrative leadership hierarchy in any successful organization, an administrator must be prepared for this so it isn't upsetting.

At some point during an educational administrator's successful reign, a subordinate or colleague will help to cause a transition of power either for her own gain or what she feels may be the greater good of the organization. Knowing that at some point this may occur, the leader must not make harsh or rash decisions to save his power base or his position in the school or district: this is exactly what the opposition wants.

Thinking this way leads to poor decision making and creates a pathway for alliances to be made that will only strengthen the attempt to take over the leader's power and what influence remains. Rather, a successful leader who recognizes or realizes that such a coup is taking shape will move the individual into a position where the decisions to be made include her at the forefront. Here, the leader actively makes the adversary part of the problem instead of being the solution.

In *Julius Caesar*, Caesar let down his guard too much, allowing Brutus to help the political takeover of his power base. The educational administrator must always be prepared for movement from others who aspire to be in his position. Again, this doesn't mean that he should make different decisions based on what may occur—just better ones.

YOU MAKE THE CALL!

You are told by a close colleague that your assistant supervisor has been talking to the rest of your team about the reading initiatives you put in place to increase the reading levels of students in the building. Your confidant explains that your assistant is telling the team that the interventions are just busy work because you have no clue about the program, and that she would give them more support and more prep time if she were the supervisor. She went on to explain that she does most of your work for you, and that she is constantly bailing you out of trouble with the central office.

Your confidant asks that you don't say anything, but he just thought you should know. He says the assistant is talking about you at every opportunity to anyone who will listen.

What are your next steps? How do you approach your assistant?

COACHES' CORNER

1. Educational leaders are only successful when they work in sync with their team. As human nature dictates, a time will come during the leader's career when an individual or group of individuals will test the leader's authority and attempt to move into her role. Discuss a time in your career when you felt that someone you trusted was undermining your authority or your decisions. How did you handle the situation? How did you respond to the individual?
2. Explain how politics plays a major role in any possible takeover situation or coup. How does a leader identify that it is happening?
3. What decisions may be affected by the situation? What strategies can you use to continue the work that needs to be done while ensuring against a takeover?

Chapter 20

Knowing When to Exit and Planning It

We have spent the previous chapters discussing the importance of building relationships, avoiding political traps, and gaining the support of stakeholder groups for a chief school administrator, superintendent, principal, director, or other school leader to gain the confidence of the community when he is making decisions that inevitably will affect the educational system. Without the support of community groups and stakeholders, including his administrative team, the school leader will have an extremely difficult time moving the mission of the district forward, and he will not increase his human and political capital, causing continued issues with future decisions, programs, and policies that he wants to put in place.

Alongside the decisions that need to be made every day in his position, the administrator must always consider the political and programmatic impact that comes with the choices he makes and how he manages constituents, employees, and staff. Strategies that he must employ, which are included in his toolbox, are designed to work with different stakeholder groups based on the needs of individual members as well as the entire group.

Educational administration is a fulfilling, interesting field. First, the daily decisions educational leaders make can effect change that can be viewed as both influential and problematic for the community they serve. As each local education agency has its own set of values with a vision and mission that sets apart one community from the next, state, federal, and contemporary issues also sometimes challenge the direction of a district or school.

Educational leaders are charged with balancing the views of the community, through the oversight of either an appointed or elected school board, with the needs of the students so each student is successful in an ever-changing global marketplace.

Although the theory seems simple, successfully putting it into practice is what sets an everyday school leader apart from a great school leader. A leader can manage the day-to-day operations as outlined by the mission, but a great school leader sets himself apart by using each decision to strengthen his position in the district or organization while impacting decisions that he will make in the future.

He does this by understanding that although simple solutions may seem relatively easy on the surface, scrubbing data trends and implementing a deeper dive to investigate the hurdles and challenges to come are the only true ways to ensure that a decision doesn't negatively affect other, unassuming stakeholder groups. In turn, he controls any political shrapnel from the decisions he makes by knowing which stakeholders and other community groups will be impacted and how this impact will affect the district, the students, and the leader himself.

A school leader also fully understands that the career field that she has chosen is political in nature. In reminding herself every day that each action may have a political attachment, she knows that she needs to be politically savvy, not political, in dealing with the daily and long-term expectations of her office. She also knows that a board or chief administrator who hires a school leader isn't the same board that fires her. Here, she recognizes that as the landscape changes over the years, along with the needs and values of the community, so may the support for the leader herself.

Thus, when one enters the field of educational administration, one must be certain to wholly understand that the day may come when it is in the best interests of all parties concerned that the school leader leaves to join another school community. If the leader understands early on that this is a possibility, then it becomes much easier for her to identify the appropriate time in her career when such a move is a viable option for both her and the community or organization she serves.

This cannot be seen as a weakness. A school leader who can evaluate, acknowledge, and pinpoint exactly when he should pack up his office and move to another community has arguably the strongest characteristic he can possess when looking inward and evaluating his strengths and weaknesses. Over time, the landscape in every educational arena will change as different families move to town, different officials are elected, and differences in ideologies and educational theory come together between the leader and his teachers, staff, and administrative team. At times, a new perspective and a fresh start can greatly boost the productivity of both the leader and the district he has served.

Again, if unpacked correctly, an administrative exit will never look like a moment of weakness or the administrator being let go without his knowledge. In fact, an educational leader who decides if and when the time is right to move allows himself to control the narrative and the exit itself. This is extremely important when considering the trajectory of his future career path and ensuring that what has been accomplished stays in place when the next leader fills his position.

It is also important that the leader does realize this will occur—someone will fill his position. Too often, young school administrators become so entrenched in their work and micromanaging specific tasks that they think that the building or district will not operate without them. Educational leaders should remind themselves from time to time that the school buildings they serve were open one hundred years before they started there, and they will be open for one hundred years after the administrator leaves. That's not to downplay or mock any efforts or positive changes that the leader has made for that community. Rather, it is a simple reminder that because administration is mandated for the safe, fair, and effective operation of every school building, the lead position must be filled by a qualified individual to ensure continuity of the educational process.

This is even more specific to the field of education and educational administration: teachers and administrators alike seem to bounce from district to district during specific points in their careers to find the correct fit for them professionally and personally. Just like the excitement when he enters the new school and community, an equal share of excitement is felt for his replacement.

So, why would a leader plan for an exit, when does a leader know to plan her exit, and how does she plan for it?

THE WHY

A great school leader understands and can accept that a time will come when he may need to leave the administrative post in his school or district. Although such a transition, on either his terms or someone else's, always brings anxiety and questions that may need to be answered, inevitably it will happen in his career. Let's face it: either through transfer, nonrenewal, retirement, or death, at some point the educational leader will leave his post.

Knowing this, one of two things ultimately will occur. First, the leader will have a plan in place to ensure that the values he has instilled, the programs he has helped to create, and the progress he has made will remain intact and operational for at least a time after he has officially left. Some things will change or be attenuated over time as new leadership puts different initiatives in place; however, it is important that the work that the stakeholders and the administrator himself accomplished remain in place for the community after the leader has left. This will help establish traditions and provide the stakeholders with an assurance that they didn't waste their time.

Conversely, if the school administrator leaves abruptly or without a prepared exit plan, all the progress he has made in the name of the district, school, organization, and community is in jeopardy of being lost. This can occur when other leaders in the district now take advantage of the absence of the leader, or as outside influencers bring their own agendas that now become part of the landscape during this state of influx.

With an exit plan in place, the programs established, personnel appointments to positions made, and other progress that was realized by the educational leader have a chance of remaining during the transition of power and throughout the tenure of the new leader.

THE WHEN

Now that the why has been established, it is important for the school leader to recognize when it is time to exit a school, district, or organization. Although this decision is not easy, or to be taken lightly, it is something that the administrator needs to understand and accept, even if it's not her decision. If the leader recognizes that she may not be renewed based on her sense of how she is being evaluated or valued in the school community, it is sometimes better to plan for an exit in a timely fashion so she can control the narrative.

Based on her ability to evaluate her own actions and the active responses of her constituent base (teachers, other administrators, students, the community at large), the school leader should consider planning her exit when several key indicators of successful leadership have changed.

Trust and Mutual Respect

A school leader can no longer lead if he perceives that he is not trusted or respected by the school community and especially, by his team. The reverse is true as well: when the leader feels that he can no longer trust those members he was once close with and respected.

COLLABORATION

A leader may consider an exit when efforts to collaborate with others on her team fail to occur on a frequent basis. Notwithstanding the fact that busy schedules and other emergencies may encroach upon the ability to meet more often, a purposeful lack of collaboration between the leader and the team creates a disconnect that will ultimately lead to disaster. When this occurs, it signals a poor level of communication between the leader and his team; at that point, usually it has gone too far for repair.

Productivity

Is the productivity of the team and the stakeholder groups inside the system suffering or nearing nonexistent? This type of outcry distinctly relates to the relationship and respect (or lack thereof) that the leader has in consideration of his team and other groups that he works with every day. If the team isn't producing results or the results are below par, the leader must look beyond his ego and realize the issues.

Employee Satisfaction

Are the district teams happy with their performance? Do they blame the leader for an inability to lead them into successful programs and environments? Does the leader ensure that outlined projects are pathways to employee satisfaction; if so, can she still get her team excited about those initiatives?

If the answer is an emphatic "no" or even "maybe," it is time for the leader to plan her exit. Employee satisfaction is the cornerstone of any truly productive work environment. Besides students, the most important players on the team in an educational system are those people in the trenches. If they are unsatisfied, the entire system needs repair.

Morale

Do individuals still aspire to work with the school leader? If this is a hard "no," then morale is strained. When gauging the morale of an administrative team or staff, it is important for any leader to understand that it must not be based on friendship or personal like/dislike of the leader. Assessing the morale in an educational setting must be done frequently and with different stakeholder groups to ensure that a professional setting is not only still operational but productive as well. Low morale leads to a stale work environment and increases animosity toward the leader. It can also cause factions to build against the leader that may undermine her role in the organization.

Everyone in the Room Knows More Than the Leader Does

As individuals on a leadership team continue to grow in their own roles, career paths, and political ties, it is inevitable that they will begin to challenge the leader, to posture for position and control. To be clear, this type of challenge stands apart from the daily disagreements or constructive suggestions that leaders engage in with one another to move an educational system forward. Differences of opinion cause important conversations to take place, which, in turn, lead to formulating ideas and promoting forward, progressive trends on learning and social and emotional awareness.

Rather, when the challenge seems disrespectful, unwarranted, and permeates an "I gotcha" atmosphere, the leader must recognize that the dissent most likely is not attached to him personally but his role as the leader. Here, his team starts to recognize that he may not be as effective as he once was, and that they are more equipped to make impactful decisions. They begin to dismiss the leader, affecting his ability to lead.

THE HOW

As important as is making the decision to leave at the appropriate time, the leader must also have a plan ready to put in place to ensure a smooth transition and preserve all that he and his colleagues have accomplished. In considering such an exit plan, the educational leader must remember two key points.

First, he must involve other members of his team by giving them direct responsibilities to ensure that they truly understand their place throughout the transition. The leader must choose strong allies for these roles, understanding that he won't physically be present when the transition takes place. Thus, he must be able to trust certain individuals to continue to carry out the responsibilities associated with such a plan and support the intended outcomes.

Next, the leader cannot make the plan complicated. As his exit will ultimately create confusion, maybe even chaos, the plan he outlined must be direct and succinct. Keeping a simple outline will ensure that the programs, personnel changes, and other additions he made in the school, district, or organization will remain when a new leader fills his position.

Announce Transition to Stakeholders

As the educational leader led under the guise of transparency, so should she remain transparent in her exit. To be clear, being transparent at this point in her career at the school or in the district does not consist of relaying the details of the reasons for the exit to the stakeholder groups. Whether it was on her terms or a board decision, a leader's position when leaving one job for the next should always include the leader humbling herself by thanking her former stakeholders for working to make the organization a better place.

The transparent part of the decision to exit should be the leader's announcement as soon as it becomes public. What this does at the very least is quell any rumors that will surface prior to the leader confirming that they are true.

Successor

Throughout a leader's tenure, he should be preparing for his exit and working to create a pipeline for a future leader to take his spot. This would be an administrative leader who holds many of the same ideals as he does and was involved in the same mission and programs that the leader helped to create.

It is also important that the leader advises his successor that he needs to create his own programs and brand as well, with the hope that the past programs and initiatives can be incorporated in future plans.

Transition of Power

A leader planning an exit must work hard to ensure that the transition goes smoothly. This may be an understandable accommodation for the leader making the exit; however, it may be difficult to get that same buy-in from the incoming administrator. This may be true especially if the exit was not mutually agreed to, the release was contested, or the board/central leadership feels disrespected based upon how the leader is choosing to exit.

Regardless, to ensure that programs remain in full consideration after he officially leaves the position, the leader must assist with the transition of power in any way possible. This may include meeting with his replacement or leaving detailed notes to help enhance initiatives.

Being Available

The most important part of any exit plan is for the leader to be available. This is where his true leadership qualities must shine, and he may need to enter an uncomfortable situation to make things occur.

Being available is different from being assertive or pushy. The leader must remember that he is no longer the administrator in that school or district; regardless of what he thinks of a decision that is made, it technically isn't his place to judge. However, what he must come to fully understand is that the more he makes himself available to the new administrator taking his position, the more influence he may have in assuring that conditions remain unchanged after he leaves.

YOU MAKE THE CALL!

Dr. Gladys Farroh has been chief school administrator for the past twelve years in the Ruby Ridge Mountain School District. She has decided to move on from education, retiring from Ridge on June 30 of this year.

Dr. Farroh has worked alongside numerous board members and central office administrators during her tenure in the district, and three internal candidates are vying to be the next CSA of the school system.

As each of the three administrators has a different and distinct leadership style, the board is having a difficult time agreeing which candidate would be best to follow Dr. Farroh in leading the schools. Several members have suggested a national search by a consulting firm to find the best fit for the position.

As Dr. Farroh has read this text, she knows how important an exit plan is and how crucial it is to pass the position to an internal candidate who can continue to enhance the programs and initiatives that she put in place over the past decade.

What are Dr. Farroh's next steps for ensuring a smooth exit from Ruby Ridge? How does Dr. Farroh persuade the board to appoint her recommendation as her successor?

COACHES' CORNER

1. It's not easy for educational leaders to think about their exit from a district, school, or organization. In fact, most administrators do not have an exit plan prepared for the time when they will be leaving their position. The point is: one day, whether she wants to or is told to, the educational leader will leave her position. Discuss a time when a leader during your professional career left his post. How was the transition? Did programs and initiatives remain after he left? Did you know who the heir apparent was and did he/she get the position?
2. What are the most important tenets of an exit plan?
3. How can a school administrator ensure that her exit plan will be followed after she leaves? What can she do if it isn't being followed? How should she react?

About the Author

Dr. Richard Tomko has had numerous administrative responsibilities during his twenty-four-year career in educational administration. He has been a building administrator at the middle and secondary levels and responsible for district-wide curriculum, assessment, innovative program initiatives, technology, and professional development while in central office positions. Dr. Tomko has dedicated his career to serving communities as an educational leader, acting as a director, assistant principal, principal, assistant superintendent, and superintendent in both private and public-school systems.

He earned a doctor of philosophy degree in educational leadership, management, and policy from Seton Hall University; a master of business administration from Johns Hopkins University; a master of jurisprudence from Loyola University of Chicago School of Law; and holds certificates in community and economic development from Pennsylvania State University and the Brain, Mind, and Teaching from Johns Hopkins University. He is an adjunct professor at Manhattan College, Montclair State University, Seton Hall University, and Centenary University, teaching in both doctoral and master's-level programs in school building leadership and counseling. He also works as a consultant to educational institutions and families.

Dr. Tomko was named Essex County New Jersey Superintendent of the Year in 2020 for exhibiting leadership for learning, communication, professionalism, and active participation in community involvement with an understanding of regional, national, and international issues. He has been honored with receiving the New Jersey State Governor's Jefferson Award for volunteerism and recognized by the U.S. Department of Defense with his receipt of the Patriot Award in 2018 and the Above and Beyond award in 2019. Most recently, Dr. Tomko was spotlighted in *Education Week* as one of eight Leaders to Learn From in 2023 for exhibiting innovative solutions to fix some of the most pressing challenges facing K–12 schools in this critical period of our history.

Dr. Tomko is a change agent for creativity and problem solving and works with administrative teams to decrease achievement gaps between demographic subgroups of learners by involving families, stakeholders, and community groups in the restoration of student engagement leading to overall student success.

www.ingramcontent.com/pod-product-compliance
Lightning Source LLC
Chambersburg PA
CBHW032215230426
43672CB00011B/2571